Practical
Feng Shui
for the Office

May you find,
and keep,
the balance in your life!

- Kathryn

Practical
Feng Shui
for the Office

Finding Your Individual Balance
in the Workplace

KATHRYN WILKING

iUniverse, Inc.
Bloomington

Practical Feng Shui for the Office
Finding Your Individual Balance in the Workplace

iUniverse books may be ordered through booksellers or by contacting:

iUniverse
1663 Liberty Drive
Bloomington, IN 47403
www.iuniverse.com
1-800-Authors (1-800-288-4677)

Because of the dynamic nature of the Internet, any web addresses or links contained in this book may have changed since publication and may no longer be valid. The views expressed in this work are solely those of the author and do not necessarily reflect the views of the publisher, and the publisher hereby disclaims any responsibility for them.

ISBN: 978-1-4759-8818-5 (sc)
ISBN: 978-1-4759-8820-8 (hc)
ISBN: 978-1-4759-8819-2 (ebk)

Library of Congress Control Number: 2013908026

Printed in the United States of America

iUniverse rev. date: 05/24/2013

My husband, Stephen Rigbey, gets the prize for being the most patient, understanding and open-minded individual. He has been tolerant through all the rants and all the discussions about feng shui, human behaviour, office politics, EMFs and this book.

In the last few years, we've driven ourselves and the dog across the country, moved three times (in three years) executed an enormous renovation, and we can still laugh together as we discuss the idiosyncrasies of life.

K

~~~

Every new adventure challenges me to be a better person.

~~~

CONTENTS

ACKNOWLEDGMENTS

- Many thanks to the team—Mia Staysko, Kelly Kaur and Janelle HarrisBorm—at the Sacred Lotus School in Calgary, Alberta, Canada.
- Dana Smithers, from PRES Staging and Resource Centre, Vancouver, British Columbia, Canada, for your commitment and support as my business coach.
- Sonia Haynes, from the Center for Innovation Studies, in North Vancouver, British Columbia, for keeping me calm, grounded and focused on my life goals.
- The amazing International Feng Shui Guild (IFSG) that continues to encourage me and many others.
- Sincere thanks to the clients and friends who have allowed me into their homes and offices with the intention to make the world a better place.

~~~

The only reason this book was written is because I had the support to begin.
Thank you!

~~~

INTRODUCTION

The purpose of this book is to take the mystery out of feng shui and show you how practical it really is. Feng shui can give you the guidance to become more aware of your surroundings and the tools to de-stress your life. For those readers who have not been exposed to feng shui, it is more than moving your furniture around. I want to present this valuable information in layman's terms and make it simple to understand.

Feng shui literally translates as "wind and water." It is about the energy and movement of things you can see and those you can't. This energy changes from day to day, season to season, year to year. These energy patterns include personal energy in yourself and in your surroundings as well as the vast energy from the cosmos. The energy force that links people with their surroundings is called *ch'i*. Translated as "cosmic breath," ch'i circulates in our bodies, around the earth and in the atmosphere. The main objective of feng shui is to enhance the environmental ch'i to improve the flow of ch'i in our bodies, thus improving the function of our lives. Harmony and balance are essential factors in feng shui, linking man and the universe.

The theory of opposites in the universe, referred to as *yin and yang*, is also part of feng shui. Yin is dark, soft and feminine, while yang is light, energetic and masculine. The impact of these influences is apparent in all aspects of our lives. The symbol for yin and yang is similar to two tadpoles intertwined with each other, each possessing a little bit of the other's qualities. Together, they are harmony.

Ch'i energy can be different depending on the individual and the environment. Your personal emotions will reflect this energy. Yin ch'i is gentle, quiet and relaxed, while yang ch'i can be aggressive, charged and passionate. To have only the energy of one is to be incomplete, so there must always be a representation of the other.

Feng shui dates back over 4,000 years to a time when the early civilizations in China were choosing burial sites for their ancestors. Their quest to find the perfect resting place for all eternity involved working intimately with the heavens, the earth and the realities of the surrounding terrain. They were also evaluating the lands far and wide in order to find the best place for their families to prosper.

Today, we are not looking for burial grounds, but still use the basic principles in feng shui to observe the environment as influenced by the factors of modern life. We look for the changing dynamics of ch'i energy by taking physics, psychology, architecture and design into consideration for analyses. This extends to the actual building design and interior room shapes, angles, colours and placement of furnishings. Within the buildings, we look at these dynamics and how they relate with the people that live and work in the buildings. Other exterior factors such as adjacent structures, freeway arteries and power lines can all come into consideration in a feng shui analyses.

The feng shui style I chose to study is the Black Hat Sect (also referred to as Black Sect Tantric Buddhism-BTB). BTB is an amalgamation of many influences; it has evolved out of the long journey of Buddhist belief from India through Tibet and China, at each place absorbing new customs, opportunities and inventions. While traditional feng shui relies heavily on a compass, I believe the progressive BTB style is a perfect fit for me and my clients in our modern world.

One of the early feng shui concepts expanded upon by the late BTB Grand Master Professor Lin Yun is the Five-Element Theory, part of which forms the basis of this book. When applied to physical elements, it is very practical and functional, but when applied to the individual, this theory becomes absolutely fascinating. The layers and layers of personality traits within us all, both positive and negative, start to make sense. This book will take you through the steps in setting up your physical workspace and then show you how to understand yourself, your coworkers and the environment around you.

Feng shui has many layers. You *can* move energy by manipulating things in the environment. And just when you think you have figured it out, something else emerges. The simple mundane *cures* and enhancements mentioned in this book are only the tip of what is possible. They are as unique as each individual. They can change with the times and are very practical. Anything that influences you can change the dynamics of your life. Through progress and modernization over thousands of years, the aim of feng shui has remained the same: the pursuit of a more comfortable and harmonious place to live and work.

Enjoy your journey on the road to an organized, productive and balanced lifestyle.

CHAPTER 1

Feng Shui Your Cubicle

I have met with so many people in the last few years who apologize for their office. Apologize? For what? They all appear to be competent, sane people with good jobs, so what is the problem? Well, a lot of them are embarrassed. They don't really like their workspace. The desk is piled high with projects or papers, and I listen to the complaint that "This office doesn't really work for me" from many of my clients.

To put you all at ease, you are *working*, right? You are allowed to have papers all over your desk; in fact, having a lot of paper can mean job security these days. The problem is really the flow, the routine and the organizing of the projects. Feng shui can help you with all of these things.

A feng shui office should give you a balanced flow of energy so you can accomplish the tasks of the day. The goal is to make your time productive and functional. Achieving that balance means different things for different people. By identifying obstacles and distractions, you can clear your space (and your mind) in order to grow. The balance in your office will be affected by the goals you have for yourself, both at the office and in your personal life.

~~~

Yin and yang are used to describe opposites in values and energy.
Yin is soft, dark, restful and feminine. Yang is hard, solid, energized and masculine.
Watch for these influences when you are evaluating your office space.

~~~

Setting Your Goals

Some companies encourage a "vision board"—a poster board or similar setup to focus on your goals, intentions and achievements. Think of your desk, or even your entire office, as your vision board. Everything you put in there must have a purpose. The adjustments to your workspace must be personal. What you see and what you think will support your life goals.

Reader Challenge

There are a few basic questions you need to ask yourself before setting your goals. Write down the goals that you have for the position you are in right now.

- How do these goals fit with the future of the company?
- What do you like about your job?
- What don't you like about your job?

When you have a vision that you can believe in, you are on your way!

~~~

If you shoot an arrow into the air, you will hit nothing. If you shoot an arrow toward a target, there is a focus.

~~~

Kathryn Wilking

The Command Position

One of the first things to consider in the office is the placement of the desk and other furniture. Regardless of whether you have an entire room designated as your office or simply a closet or cubicle, you will need to find the Command Position. This would be the best spot to place your desk in order to see the whole room and the doorway, yet not be in direct alignment with the doorway. In your Command Position, you should feel comfortable and relaxed. If you feel good sitting at your desk, it is a good indication that you are on the right track. You may not feel like a success right away, but you will enjoy the process of becoming successful in the future.

The Command Position and its complexities refer back to an ancient Chinese model, as explained in Appendix A. When you find your Command Position, you automatically become safe (your back is protected), you have control (have your sight lines defined) and you are out of the way of distractions.

Things to think about when setting up your work area in Command Position:

- When you sit with your back to a door or open space, your subconscious could be wondering what is going on behind your back. Try to get creative with your desk arrangement so you can see the door from your desk.
- If you cannot find a Command Position that faces the door, consider placing a small mirror (purse-size or convex) discreetly on your desk to face the doorway. This way, if someone's shadow crosses the light behind you, there will be no surprise. (Avoid having the mirror reflecting directly on your actual work. This could give you the impression that you have even more work to complete.)
- If possible, you will want to avoid sitting with a window behind you. The window is clear and fragile and will not give you grounding or support for your back. A curtain in

4

a light fabric or a screen divider should be considered to make you feel more secure. A floor plant behind you can also act as a barrier, if your company will allow items that are not bolted down.

- A low bookshelf or credenza behind you may give you security, but a high bookshelf, even fixed to the wall, can give you the feeling of being overwhelmed (too much work to do, being buried). Even the subconscious thought of *What if something falls?* This could distract your productivity.
- Do not place your desk under a beam or at the side of a room where the ceiling slopes down behind you. Any configuration that makes you feel anxious, overwhelmed or stifled should be reconsidered. Try to just sit at your desk for a few minutes to see if any of these issues are present.

Tip: A manager should sit in the most commanding position to assert authority with his or her team. If the boss sits too close to the door, he risks being constantly interrupted. Being involved with the smaller issues of the day, he could be treated with less respect.

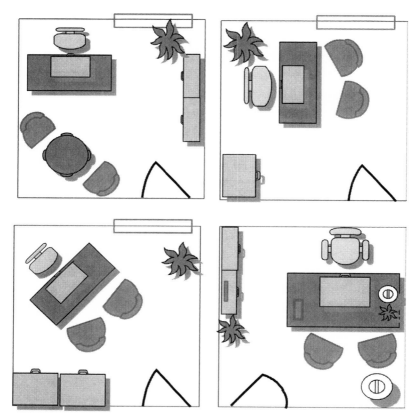

Figure 1.1 These desks are all in the Command Position. The people that work here will have the best range of vision and can avoid being startled or distracted during the day. Sitting with one's back to a door, even a fire door, can bring uncertainty. Feng Shui Masters would label this 'bad luck'.

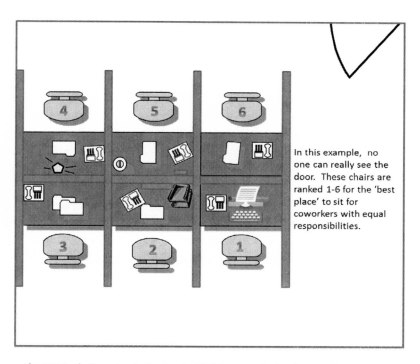

In this example, no one can really see the door. These chairs are ranked 1-6 for the 'best place' to sit for coworkers with equal responsibilities.

Figure 1.2 If a Team Leader is placed with this group, the Leader may choose desk #3 as his 'best place' to sit in command. This would allow for more control and less interruptions for the Leader.

Anyone may find it stressful to sit directly across from the boss, or any person who is particularly bothersome. Place a quality, crystal paperweight or candleholder on the desk between the two positions to create a better atmosphere. See desk #4.

Is There a Best Place for My Desk?

Modern businesses tend to maximize their employee capacity by setting up little pods, or cubicles grouped together, for their workstations. Many workstations are set up for the employee to face a wall or partition. Originally, this was to provide privacy and avoid distractions in an open-concept facility. In reality, you are working in a closet, and you are unable to see what is going on. Not too long ago, an acceptable punishment for a child was to send him to a corner, nose to the wall. From there, he could not see anyone or find out what was going on. Do you ever feel punished or out of touch in your cubicle?

Take these factors into consideration when evaluating your cubicle's feng shui:

- If your workstation faces another person without a divider, this will only work if you are compatible or you are working on the same project. You may be more productive if you turn the desks out a one-quarter turn to give yourself personal space and still be recognized as part of the team.
- If you are stationed at the end of a long hallway, you'll have other concerns. Long hallways can become stagnant, without enough fresh air reaching the desk—or the opposite, with full-force energy streaming toward you.
- Indoor air quality is another potential problem. Also check for good lighting, sounds, odours, heating and A/C. Make sure your space is a comfortable zone for you to work in.
- Pay attention to vacant cubicles or dead space. These areas can collect clutter and become stagnant energy. I've seen more than one empty desk become a dumping ground for office supplies and brochures. If the vacant desk appears to be a better position for you, clean it up and move in. Give yourself a fresh start. If the vacant desk is beside you, you can try to keep it clear (for new staff

or visitors) or bring in some bright objects and plants for your desk to balance out the dead space.

- Check out the traffic flow in the room. Are you situated just off the bathroom door, lunch room or break room? All this additional traffic can distract you from your work. (See figure 1.4.)

- Look for poison arrows. A poison arrow is a perceived line drawn from a corner or sharp edge that points directly toward you. Arrows can also show up in other ways. Pay attention to your view when you enter a room or look up from your desk. If the view is split—one eye focused on long distance and the other near—your brain needs to process this every time you look up. This very simple issue could be the main thing sabotaging the quality of your work. (See figure 1.5.)

- Electromagnetic fields (EMFs) are of concern in modern offices. With unlimited wireless pulses from our devices (and everyone else's), some people can become fatigued from the nonstop activity on our brains and bodies. Be aware of these EMFs. Every wireless phone, computer, printer, mouse and more all carry their own wave. Research on this topic is still new, and we don't have the answers to all the questions. Be aware of your environment. For further reading on this subject, check out the recommended reading in Appendix D.

This may appear to be a lot of trivial detail to deal with at the office. I understand. Not everyone is sensitive to all of these issues. If it doesn't bother you having your desk under a large beam, that is just fine. But if you are unhappy, unproductive and feeling bogged down most days, you might want to try moving your desk.

Is there a best place for your desk? Absolutely! In an ideal world, you could choose the perfect spot for yourself. But in tight quarters or as part of a huge company, you may need to get a little creative in order to find the best place.

The bottom line is; you need to feel comfortable with the direction the cubicle is facing for this space to work. If you can find a spot where you can be happy, have some natural light, enjoy a little privacy and still be aware what is going on, you will be set up for success!

Choosing Your Desk and Chair

A solid desk is a powerful tool. You don't want to choose a desk that is weak in any way. Poor choices include any desk that is wobbly, lacking support, propped up or made of glass.

- If your desk is sturdy, it will give you support.
- If your desk is large, you will feel confident and competent to move with energy in your endeavours.
- If your desk is too small and tight, you may underestimate your goals and achievements.
- If your desk was previously owned by a successful individual who you respect, good feelings will bring you good benefits.
- Give the same attention in choosing your desk chair as you have given to selecting your desk. A chair with armrests will provide you with strength and securities, helping you stay strong in the Command Position. Check for free rotation of the wheels and height adjustments to find a proper fit.

A Few Words about Clutter

A cluttered desk can be the most unproductive desk. I know: we all get busy. It is too common to see a desk cluttered with projects in progress, unpaid bills and things to file all mixed up together.

The piles of projects in progress actually have good energy! It is okay to have them out on the desk. They represent a task, fulfillment, the puzzle, the work order and money (the reward for a job well done.) It is the unfinished projects that gather the dust, destroy the energy on the desk and deplete the motivation necessary to finish the task. These are the items that need to get moved *off* the desk and into another area: file box, file folder, trash or the desk of someone you delegate it too.

Do not jeopardize your efficiency by procrastinating about what to do with the dead files on your desk.

- Clean, clean, clean!
- Try to keep the desk free of clutter directly in front of where you sit. This actually encourages you to sit at your desk.
- Having a desk blotter designating your prime work area can help you focus your attention in that spot. When you are finished with a file, move it off to the side to give your complete attention to the next task.
- It would be helpful to designate one area or side of your desk to the incoming issues and the other side for outgoing or completed items to file, send or delegate to others. Coordinate this in-out flow with your team, partner or administrative assistant.

As soon as you get the paper clutter sorted out, you'll be able to find new opportunities.

Tip: While you are rearranging your desk, be sure to clear out the drawers. Get into the little corners and little bits of boxes and things, too. Anything that is dead, dying, stale, forgotten or redundant should be removed. All of these items have potential to block your creativity. When you are finished, you will notice a huge weight has been lifted. Don't allow anyone else to clear your desk. This is your space.

Office Decor

Office decoration can determine your mood and motivation. Choose all your pictures, artwork and items carefully so that they actually reflect your goals and intentions. Items that inspire you will uplift your spirit and remind you of your goals and successes, regardless of whether you have a private office or shared space.

The images that you choose to decorate your space can be aggressive and racy or very gentle and calm. The tone of these images will set the mood in your office. Refer back to yin and yang; as they are opposites in the universe, you need to be aware of their impact. What do you need for your type of work? A sales office may need something more aggressive, while a calmer image would likely be more appropriate for a doctors' office.

Tip: When you are ready to go shopping, bring along anything that inspires you—postcards, magazines, a pillowcase, scarves, sweaters or paint swatches. You already know your favourite colours and textures, so get them working for you.

If you need to stay energized, witty and inspired, you'll need yang energy. Yang energy is produced by utilizing hard surfaces and sharp, shiny or reflective items in your environment. This stimulation can keep you motivated through your work day. Yin energy should be introduced when you require a slower pace, such as a time when you are contemplating a solution or editing a newsletter. A slower work style could benefit from textiles, such as drapery, chair cushions and more. Often, a large heavy object or sculpture can help settle you into a project. You need to select each item specifically for your personal needs for the space.

Take the following considerations into account:

- Maybe you like to travel. A map of the world could be related to your travel goals, a measurement of success, or it could be a total distraction, leading you to envision all the places in the world you could never possibly visit.
- Moving or rushing water on a poster can represent a busy, multitasking office or an endless outpouring of

energy—exhilarating for some, very exhausting for others.

- For less stimulation, artwork showing a tranquil lake or larger body of water could provide a solid foundation for clarity of thought and security for the group.
- A poster of anger and fighting will not encourage group efforts.
- A moody landscape will probably not help you meet deadlines.

Another point to consider is that the image on the print in front of you may have a different effect when hanging behind you. As an example, a majestic mountain hanging behind you can feel like a rock, making you feel secure, grounded and confident in your position. The same mountain hanging in front of you could be overwhelming, suggesting that you've set your goals too high, you have mountains to climb or you'll never get there because you're too tired.

Whatever you choose, it should be fabulous! It must inspire you and represent the goals and intentions you have set out. As you grow in your position, you may be drawn to different images as the years move along. Be sure to participate if others are choosing your furnishings.

Reader Challenge

Take a few minutes to identify the distractions in your office. The longer you've been in the space, the harder it is to identify those distractions. If you aren't inspired by one or more of your furnishings, it is time to set it aside and replace it with something that works for you. Ask yourself: *Does this office inspire me to be productive every day?* Open yourself and your space to experience new horizons and growth.

The Meeting: Where Do I Need to Sit?

Outside of your cubicle, common areas have their own feng shui considerations. When heading into meeting rooms, waiting areas in reception or even a restaurant, arriving early always gives you the advantage. Choose a seat where you can see the entire room and the door, so there will be no surprises.

The chairman or manager running the meeting usually sits at the head of the meeting table. Choose to sit on one side of the speaker or the other, while still being able to see the door. All eyes will be on the presentation and therefore you will be seen as important too. On the opposite end of the table, the person closest to the door may be distracted with interruptions. This individual could be the one designated to gather forgotten supplies, take messages, check the lights and so on.

Plan ahead and choose your seat. When you find the spot where you feel grounded, focused and productive, you will be in the best position for success.

Check out meeting rooms and their patterns on the next pages.

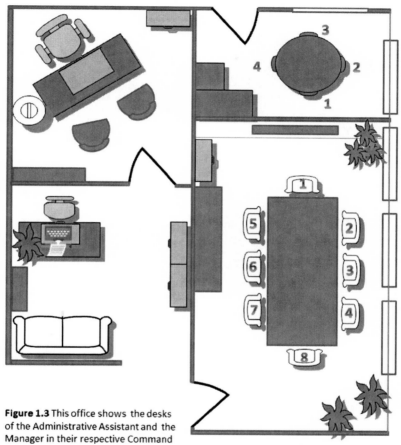

Figure 1.3 This office shows the desks of the Administrative Assistant and the Manager in their respective Command Positions. The Meeting Room and the Break Room show the best places to sit (starting with 1) in order to see the doorway and still be in command.

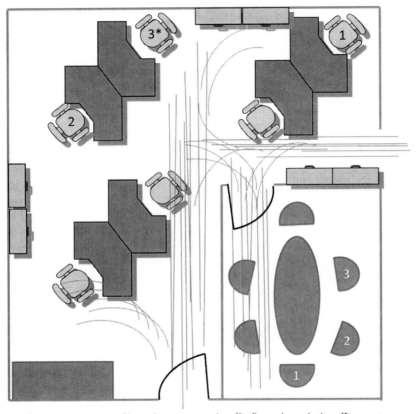

Figure 1.4 Be aware of how the energy and traffic flows through the office; not just the fans overhead, but disruptive energy coming in from the elevators, the lunch room and customer traffic. Best places to sit: Seats 1,2 or 3 as shown in both the closed office and in open concept. A few well placed room dividers could make this space more productive.

* This seat gives the most complete view of the office, but depending on the amount of traffic, may be adversely affected by traffic energy.

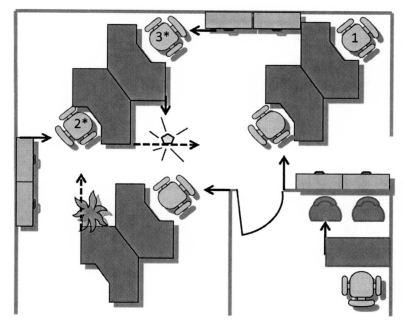

Figure 1.5 Poison arrows are the result of poor alignment in the office layout. Watch for any sharp edge pointing towards you from any direction: a doorway, desk corner, cabinet, pillar or any piece of furniture. To 'cure' a poison arrow, either rearrange the furniture or utilize a plant, lamp, or a room divider to soften the sharp edge. Alternatively, hang a well-placed wind chime or a crystal to diffuse the arrow.

If poison arrows are not bothersome to you, have another look a month from now and check again. Be aware of their presence, as these distractions can affect your peak performance, and induce anxiety.

* Seats #2 and #3 both have corners of filing cabinets immediately at their backs. A crowded workspace will add to the anxiety.

CHAPTER 2

Inside the Box

When you have your desk in the Command Position and a few accessories selected, we can add another tool to help you focus on your objective: the ba-gua. By applying the principles of the ba-gua to your space, you can get that space working for you.

Tools to Help: the Ba-gua

The BTB ba-gua is a layout or grid that is used to divide any area into nine sub-areas. This is sometimes viewed as an *energy map*—a map of nine life areas (or fortunes):

1. Family
2. Wealth and abundance
3. Fame
4. Relationships
5. Children and creativity
6. Helpful people and travel
7. Careers
8. Knowledge and self-cultivation
9. Health

The ba-gua has infinite applications, and we can only address a few in this book. Although it is often shown as an octagon, I'll be representing the ba-gua in the form of a grid for ease of use in your office layouts.

The Ba'gua

WEALTH AND ABUNDANCE *green tall plants* X Wood Element	FAME AND REPUTATION *red triangle sharp candle pointed obj* Fire Element	RELATIONSHIPS AND PARTNERSHIPS *family pic* Earth Element
FAMILY Wood Element	HEALTH AND VITALITY  Earth Element	CHILDREN AND CREATIVITY Metal Element
KNOWLEDGE AND WISDOM Earth Element	CAREER AND LIFE PATH *blue or black wavy* X *water* Water Element	HELPFUL PEOPLE AND TRAVEL Metal Element

office and desk

door

Figure 2.1 Where is the door to your space? Line up the entrance along this side.
For your desk, line this up from your chair where you normally sit.

Feng shui consultants will superimpose the ba-gua onto just about anything: rooms, buildings and building lots, a floor plan of a house or office, a specific room, a piece of furniture and more. They can use this tool to interpret what is going on in a person's life and relate any cures or enhancements for the area. The application is fairly simple. If a businessman wants to improve his finances, he may want to enhance the wealth area of his office and home. To support this goal, he may choose to enhance the fame and career areas as well.

Notes: The ba-gua is sometimes pronounced as pa-gua or ba kua. The word *gua* translates to "area" or "space." There are other sects that have different interpretations of the ba-gua not discussed in this book. Appendix B has further insights about the ba-gua.

The placement of the ba-gua for your desk or a specific object: Line the bottom edge of the grid to the edge of the desk where you sit. Regardless of what shape or size your desk is, divide your desk into nine areas—three equal parts horizontally and vertically. Make a note as to where your strongest and weakest areas are located and what is in these areas.

When placed over a larger area, your entire work area or floor of the building, the ba-gua is lined up the same: Orient the bottom line with the doorway or entrance to the area. Defining the entrance is very important. This area is extremely auspicious, as it is often referred to as the "mouth of ch'i." If your entrance to any space is blocked or cluttered, chances are the ch'i energy is not able to fully circulate in that space. When people describe their problems or issues as indecision, procrastination or lack of fulfillment, an easy cure is to clear the entrance area.

The idea is to identify and reinforce those areas where needed. Each gua relates to a particular life area. Each life area is defined with its own element, colour, shape, number, season and more. I cannot tell you specifically what you need in each area, as each area should be personally accented by *you*, with things that are important to *you*!

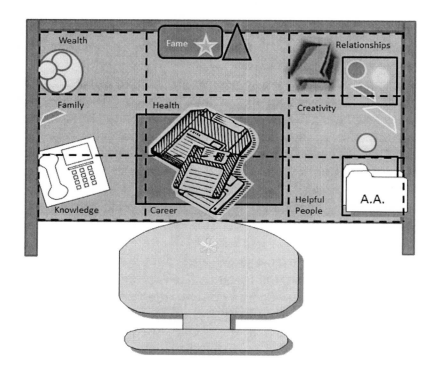

Figure 2.2 A simple Ba'qua placed on a desk shows the positions of your Nine Life Areas. In order for you to work on your goals, reinforce these life areas with specific enhancements relevant to you.
i.e. place Wealth goals in the far left, Fame and Recognition items in the center, and Relationship goals in the far right corner.

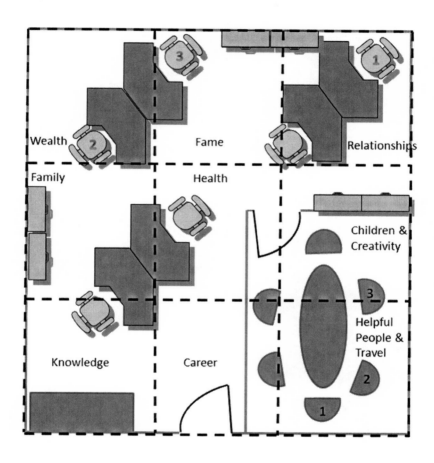

Figure 2.3 This Ba'gua is applied to a small business office. Each area is available for enhancements, depending on the goals or intentions set by the shared office.

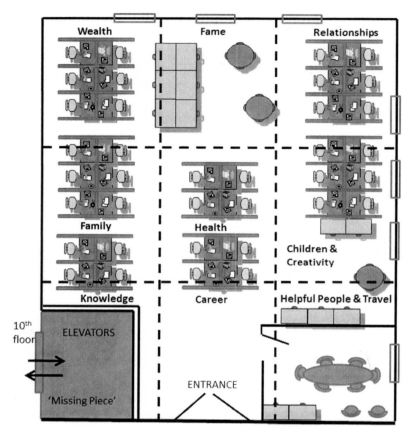

Wealth | Fame | Relationships

Family | Health | Children & Creativity

Knowledge | Career | Helpful People & Travel

10th floor | ELEVATORS

'Missing Piece'

ENTRANCE

Figure 2.4 This Ba'gua is applied to an entire office floor. All of these life areas could be 'enhanced' in order to support the office goals. There are two major issues with this office space. The Career Area in the entrance is not grounded as it is totally void of reinforcements. Also, this floor is missing a large piece of the Knowledge Area where the elevators are located. Refer to Appendix B regarding 'missing pieces'.

Tools to Help: The Five Elements

We can use the Five-Element Theory in feng shui to relate tangible objects in your office, such as your desk and the furnishings, to the different elements depending on their colour, shape and more. To get you started thinking in these terms, listed below are a few examples of the elements and what they represent:

1. Wood
    - colour: green
    - shape: thin and tall
    - season: spring
    - objects: tall plants, tall carvings, tall lamps, images of leaves or plants

2. Fire
    - colour: red
    - shape: triangle and sharp
    - season: summer
    - objects: candles, pointed objects, red everything, actual fire, bling

3. Earth
    - colour: tan, yellow, caramel, clay, rust, brown
    - shape: squares and rectangles
    - season: late summer
    - objects: clay pots or dishes, tumbled stones, dirt or earth, granite, stones, rocks

4. Metal
    - colour: white and grey
    - shape: oval or round
    - season: autumn
    - objects: glass, mirrors, round dishes, brass pots, gold and silver jewellery, metal sculptures

5. Water
    - colour: dark blue or black
    - shape: wavy
    - season: winter
    - objects: actual water, fountains, wavy patterns in floor mats, book covers or knick-knacks

Some items can represent more than one element or amplify the representation of that element. For example, a round blue vase can represent both metal and water. A red candle can represent double the fire. A clay bowl with glass stones and a tea light can represent earth, metal and fire. A glass vase with water and tall flowers can represent water, metal and wood.

The Nine Areas of Life

We can now use the two tools, the ba-gua and the five elements, to get you started in understanding how to improve your physical workspace. The five elements are placed onto the ba-gua in a specific order, with each element connected with a different life area. Refer back to Figure 2.1. These elements can be used to support your goals in each life area.

The *family area* is associated with strength. Family dynamics include forming foundations within the corporate family as well as creating a solid heritage. Honesty, trust and reliability are crucial for a family in order to leave a legacy. This area is associated with the wood element, as it is constantly growing and changing. Tall columns, trees and plants all support the wood element and growing, solid relationships. The following suggestions can help you strengthen your family area:

- Display activities or projects that support team spirit and encourage participation.
- Green is the colour for growth. Green in general is a soothing, supportive colour.

- Tall is the shape—use floor lamps, flagpoles, tall ferns or vertical stripes.
- Support this area with anything made from wood, including tables, chairs, lamps, bowls or carvings.

The (wealth and abundance area) is also associated with the wood element, tall columnar shapes, and the colours green and red. The wood element and its growth is stronger in the spring when the air is fresh and the vegetation all around you is bursting with tremendous energy. By bringing in tall items, you can reinforce the growth and abundance energy in your world. Also refer to the family area above. The following suggestions can help you strengthen your wealth and abundance area:

- This is a great area for a plant. Ideally, you want something tall and, if possible, enhanced with a flower, berry or the colour red. If you are not a plant person, consider a good fake plant. Silk flowers or nicely made synthetics can represent the image of plants and growth. Please do not consider placing dried or "dead" flowers at your desk.
- Other items that represent wealth include anything of value to *you*, monetarily or sentimentally, that represents the cause. Options may include antiques, coins, pictures or carvings and artwork.
- Another option is to look ahead. Place a picture of where you want to take your next vacation or something that could motivate you to fulfill a goal, such as buying a boat, going fishing or travelling. Choose your own goal but put some sort of incentive in your corner.
- Refer to chapter 8, "Finding the Wealth," for more depth and specifics.

The *fame and reputation area* not only represents personal achievements, it can reflect your reputation in the world by others. Fame is associated with the fire element. You can have a strong fame area even if you feel you are very humble. The colour red is dominant in this area. The triangle shape is used here and includes other pointed or sharp shapes. The following suggestions can help you strengthen your fame and reputation area:

- Use this area to display any and your most recent items of achievement. Some certificates have a red seal on them (bonus), or you may like to display them in a red frame. Display any achievements you have earned. Get them out of the drawers and into your space.
- Animals are representative of the fire element, as they are alive and perhaps untamed. You may use animal prints, textiles or photos in this area.
- Anything with a triangular shape will represent the fire element. Some clocks come in a triangle shape, candles (they represent actual fire, right?), plants with a triangular leaf, a Kleenex box with a sharp design or a sailboat—it's all good!

The relationship area generally refers to your personal life. At work, this area affects your close working relationships with your coworkers or partners. It is obviously important to keep this area strong. The relationship area is associated with the earth element and the shape of squares and rectangles. A key word here is *receptive*: Whether you are looking for a relationship or are in a relationship, you need to be able to give and receive. The following suggestions can help you strengthen your relationship area:

- This is a great area to display any earth-type objects. Things like clay pots, ceramic coffee mugs, tumbled stones or even a combination of a few things will work. Incorporate these items into holders for pens and office supplies.
- Square items work well in this area, such as file folders or file boxes. Colours to use would be anything tan, caramel,

rust, clay or brown. Think of autumn colours. The dark brown colour can remind us of solidity, grounding or hibernation.

- If you're married, it is important to have a photo of you and your partner—and *only* the two of you. This is validation that you are connected to one another and a reminder that you have support on this planet. Be aware that if you have a picture of only your partner, you may feel guilty seeing him or her alone at home waiting for you. Place family pictures on the other side of the desk in the family area and travel memorabilia in the travel area (or take those items home).

- If you are looking for a companion or strength in an existing relationship, the key number is *two*. Try to set up items in twos: two pictures, two things in a picture, two file folders, two plants, two candles, two . . . you get it. This gets your brain thinking and referring to *two* rather than *one*.

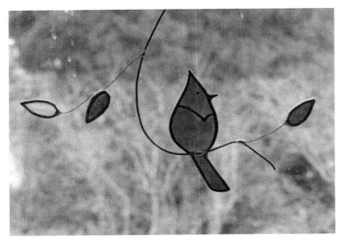

Stained glass hanging in a window can refract light and gather attention. This little red bird would enhance the wealth or fame areas. For the relationship area, you would need two birds.

Live fish or a representation of fish are auspicious in business. Ceramic fish on a wall can strengthen your wealth area and your career.

Figure 2.5a Enhancements

Silk flowers in a ceramic dish, enhanced with two round crystals can support your health, family, wealth, relationship and career life areas. Be sure to use two flowers in the relationship area.

A representative of all five elements is recommended for your health area. The silk flower: wood. The ceramic dish: earth. The tea light: fire. The glass and metal balls: metal. The blue place mat: water

Figure 2.5b Enhancements

Arrange similar objects that have different heights. Displaying groups of ceramics and porcelain can strengthen your earth areas: relationships, health and knowledge.

The round features can support your metal area, while the wavy lines can support your career. When filled with stones or glass, the earth area will become stronger. If a vase is red and filled with flowers or coins, the wealth area will be further enhanced. Get creative with your enhancements!

Figure 2.5c Enhancements

The *children and creativity area* helps you find joy in your life. This area is intended to bring out your playful side and your imagination. It is associated with the colours white or grey, circular shapes and all types of metal. The metal element is also represented by glass, mirrors and shiny surfaces. If you don't have children, there is still your inner child to play with. You need to have fun, find creative ways to solve daily puzzles and manoeuvre through the obstacles of life. The following suggestions can help you strengthen the children and creativity area:

- This is a great place to display artwork or other achievements by you or your child.
- The colours grey and white represent a blank canvas on which to create. Just as a chef displays culinary creations on a white plate, an artist uses a blank canvas and a doctor wears a white coat, white helps you maintain a neutral, open mind.
- Other enhancements you can use for reinforcing this area are brass pots, mirrors (round and metal), handmade objects or circular patterns on textiles or a rug.

The *helpful-people and travel area* is also associated with the metal element. This is one of the most interactive areas, where you relate to the outside world and your clients. Think of a time when you were travelling and you needed help. Think of a time where you did a "good deed for the day." It is a great feeling. Where would we be without interaction with other humans? Remember, what goes around comes around. The following suggestions can help you strengthen your helpful-people and travel area:

- This is the place to collect items to delegate to others. Your administrative assistant, if you are lucky enough to have one, can process the files and correspondence. These items should be placed on the extreme lower right of your desk or your office.

- If you have a spiritual nature, the lower right section of your office or desk is also the best place for religious books or pictures.
- This is a location for your affirmations or gifts from a mentor. Photographs of places you've travelled can also be displayed in this area.
- Placing your upcoming itinerary and plane tickets here in your desk drawer can ensure you meet the right people at the right time at your destination.

Vacation shots and souvenirs are fun. Display them either in the
Travel area or any other area that makes sense to you.

Figure 2.6 Travel Enhancements

The career and life-path area is something you need to do alone. It involves direction, fulfillment and inner exploration to find your career path. It is as individual as each day. This is associated with the water element and is intended, like deep water, to slow you down and allow you to explore the unfolding of your destiny. Courage is the key word. It takes courage to wander off the beaten track, try something new and follow the career path that calls to you. The following suggestions can help you strengthen your career and life-path area:

- Firm grounding is important. At your desk, use a blotter. In your office, check that your chair moves easily and your feet are not blocked by stuff under your desk. At your front entrance, put down a new dark blue or black welcome mat.
- Use water-element features to enhance this area. Think about stability in your choices. This is the spot for water that is contained, such as a desk fountain or aquarium. You could also choose artwork depicting bodies of water: pools, lakes and ocean. This is *not* the spot for rushing or moving water, such as a raging river.
- Other items can feature a wavy pattern—on a vase, a floor mat or textiles.
- Depending on which sector you are working in, clothes do make an impression for your career. A dark suit and white shirt is still part of "dress for success." Check out "Finding the Wealth" in Chapter 8 for more details.

The knowledge and self-cultivation area transforms your knowledge and adventures into wisdom. To be wise, you need quiet time to balance your active time, to honour the full rhythm of life. This area is associated with the earth element, which encompasses grounding, logic and nurturing. It is represented by the square and rectangular shapes as well as the earth colours. Blue is added into this area for clarity and quietness. The following suggestions can help you strengthen your knowledge and self-cultivation area:

- This is the best place for a library or a bookshelf. Books, CDs and resource materials that you are currently studying are all square-shaped, and they all contain knowledge. Don't keep them hanging around long after they are useful. Pass them along before their condition deteriorates.
- Set up a desk or reading area in this corner of the office where you can spread out a map or floor plans and engage with your projects.
- Clay pots, tumbled stones and natural sculptures utilize the earth element and fit here nicely. Any type of gem or mineral (earth-related) can be displayed here.
- Display art that portrays strong mountains, quiet places and pictures of people you consider to be accomplished.

The *health area* is in the middle of everything. This makes logical sense, because without your health, you do not have the energy to live purposefully. Health is associated with the earth element. To strengthen this area, use colours of the earth spectrum that feel good to you. The square or rectangle shape is important to utilize, as it defines a balanced area. Earth can be represented with clay, granite, slate and tumbled stones or dirt. Wear earth colours in any spectrum of tan, caramel, rust, clay and brown. Ideally, this area should be represented by all of the five elements. The following suggestions can help you strengthen your health area:

- Yellow is a great colour for morale. You can add this into your day by using yellow sticky notes (you'll never lose them), yellow notepads or file folders.
- A greeting card with a picture of flowers or birds is another idea; anything that depicts life, vitality and good health. You can tape it down flat on your desk in your

health area or even incorporate an image into your mouse pad.
- Choose a bright, lively cushion for your chair. A favourite coffee mug can give you a supportive message.
- Place an arrangement on your desk that represents all five elements. More on this is in chapter 8.

The suggestions above are easy, tangible modifications that organize and balance the chi energy in your space. It's best not to work on all nine areas of life at one time. By working on two to three related areas, you can create the momentum required to make a change. Some suggestions would be to work on the career and wealth areas together, or relationships and family. Whatever you decide to work on first is fine. This is not magic; it is positive and progressive. The energy you use to make clear intentions for change will be noticed by someone out there, and this alone will be a positive influence. The rewards will come.

The intent is to find a level of balance in your life areas. Write yourself a note to check into your life areas regularly and make any adjustments in order to meet your goals. The world is constantly moving and shifting, and you need to respond to the shifts.

The successes in your office world will be affected by the goals you have for yourself both at the office and in your personal life. When you make a decision with intention for change, you will change the energy. Don't be surprised if some exciting changes start to happen.

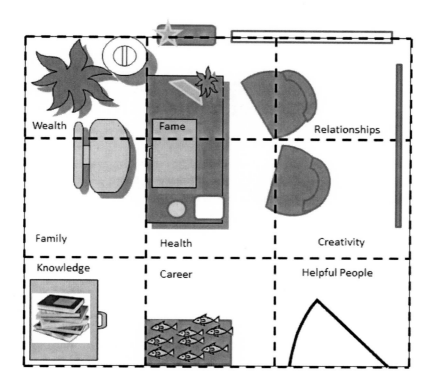

Wealth

Fame

Relationships

Family

Health

Creativity

Knowledge

Career

Helpful People

Figure 2.7 This Ba'qua is applied to a personal office. The manager of this office has enhanced her Wealth and Career Areas to help support her goals. Many of the other areas are also reinforced. The Wealth Area, a *Wood-element,* has a tall plant and a tall lamp. The Career Area is a *Water-element,* therefore, an aquarium is a fabulous choice. The Fame Area has her achievements and awards displayed on the wall. The Knowledge Area is supported by a book shelf and square shapes. The artwork in Relationships/Creativity is calming and supports her personal goals.

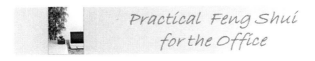

CHAPTER 3

The Personal Element Profile

When we are on top of the world and things are going great, we can relate to being "in our element." Is it rare for you to experience a good day? For some people, the answer is no. They are the lucky ones who seem to have a great job and a wonderful spouse and have it all together. Others, the ones who are stressed or struggling, do a recap of the day and promise to try to do better. But by simply figuring out who said what and who is to blame, they are still not completely solving the problem.

Balancing your life starts with learning who you are and how you fit in. You need to know how to choose your position, how you fit into the team and how to choose your team or partner. It is time to expand your new knowledge of the five elements with a good look at your habits and patterns. The five elements have great significance in feng shui. They are usually arranged in a specific order and logically relate to our Western world. They are each assigned an auspicious number, a colour, a body part, a shape, a season, a personality and more.

As you saw in the last chapter, the five elements relate to the basic components defined in feng shui: wood, fire, earth, metal and water. Their unique strengths and properties can help you manoeuvre through your day. When you have determined your dominant element, you can start looking at more characteristics of this element to influence and support your life. This can include selecting colours and patterns for your wardrobe, choosing homes and possessions that resonate with you and influencing sales teams and discussions with employees.

The Personal Element Profile (PEP) quiz in this chapter was initially designed as a game when I was asked to speak about feng shui to ladies' groups. It is a great icebreaker. This self-profile quiz seems to get people talking and chuckling with each other about their idiosyncrasies. It puts everyone in a good mood.

You'll need to take the PEP test to determine a starting point to find your dominant element. As there are no right or wrong answers, you may find that your dominant element will validate your actions in the way you respond to others. It is very common to find that your "home element" is different from your "working element." Having that awareness helps you define your friends at different times and gives you realistic objectives to strive for in the future. You may find areas for self-improvement. Or perhaps you'll find that you are well-rounded and able to change your behaviour pattern with a particular person or situation.

By identifying our individualities, we could be in our element more often. We can all learn to have good days. Could it be possible that we, on the planet Earth, could be in our element every day? Could we all learn to get along with everyone else?

Please take the time to finish the PEP quiz before you read further. This is a preliminary evaluation only, and as you read more, you will fine-tune the evaluation of yourself. You will use your new knowledge of the elements later on in this book.

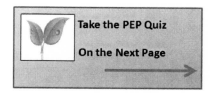

Take the PEP Quiz

On the Next Page

Do you know your *Personal Element Profile*?

According to Feng Shui, your personality can be related to one of these **Five Elements**. These lists can indicate your strengths in one area or another. Check all that applies to your to find your dominant element! Can you see any friends or coworkers?

WOOD

- ○ Flexible Schedule
- ○ Gets things done quickly
- ○ Loves a challenge
- ✓ Goal Oriented
- ○ Can be Impulsive
- ○ Enjoys a change in routine
- ✓ Confident
- ○ Thinks BIG
- ✓ Impatient; "Get to the point!"
- ✓ Likes to wear green

FIRE

- ○ Life of the Party
- ○ Thinks outside the Box
- ✓ Takes control of any problem
- ○ Animated and creative
- ○ Relaxed approach to life
- ○ Makes friends easily
- ○ Wide social circle
- ○ Passionate about life
- ○ Drama Queen at times
- ○ Loves to decorate for the holidays

EARTH

- ○ Well grounded
- ✓ Reliable and trustworthy
- ✓ Happy to Compromise
- ○ Great Nurturer
- ○ Great Mediator
- ✓ Asks a lot of Questions
- ✓ THE contact for family and friends; the nucleus
- ✓ Compiler of people and details/bills/history/facts
- ○ Protective of family
- ○ Likes to wear earth tones

METAL

- ✓ Precise thinker
- ○ Sense of Justice
- ○ Speaks UP
- ✓ Follows the Rules
- ✓ Strong Morals
- ○ Thinks in B&W, no compromising
- ✓ Has systems in place; wills/bills/security
- ○ All furniture/objects are squared off neatly
- ✓ Sense of humour is lacking
- ○ Does not like to hug

WATER

- ○ Wise, pontificating
- ○ Excels in specialized knowledge
- ○ Very smart and well read
- ○ Seeks the truth, a visionary
- ○ Reflective
- ✓ Solitary, loner
- ○ Sly sense of humour; blunt/cruel
- ○ Secretive, private person
- ○ Eccentric, anti-social
- ○ Armchair Traveller

TOTALS

WOOD __4__

FIRE __1__

EARTH __5__

METAL __5__

WATER __1__

There are no right or wrong answers to this quiz.

The Element with the highest score should be your Dominant Element. Lower scores in other areas will show you have a talent to embrace a wide range of characteristics, which in turn will help make you become a well – rounded individual.

Being a unique character, you have a unique way of getting what you want in this world!

CHAPTER 4

In Your Element

~~~

The five-element colors are an ordered sequence . . . based on natural elements that can either generate or destroy one another.
—from *Living Color: Master Lin Yun's Guide to Feng Shui and the Art of Color*

~~~ wood earth metal

When you've completed the Personal Element Profile, you should have a starting point as to what your dominant element could be. If you find yourself spread across more than one element, it indicates you are flexible in different situations. For example, if you think your dominant element is metal, you can still have characteristics that show up in the wood profile. You may also find your dominant element at work is very different from the one at home.

When you find yourself confident, fulfilled, productive, energized and generally happy in a situation, take note. You're in your element, and *that* is where you need to be. We all naturally gravitate toward our comfort zone, where our natural talents lie and things are easy for us. By identifying your strengths and weaknesses in various areas, you can work toward a balance to be in your element. The results can be extremely rewarding.

This chapter is going to give you more details on the five elements so that you can identify different personality traits in your friends and coworkers. As you continue to look around and figure out what makes you tick, you can see why your relationships with some people are very different from others. By taking the time to identify the elements of the people around you, you will be able to connect patterns in your behaviour with certain element types. Learning how to get along with everyone is an acquired skill. Once you attain it, you can manoeuvre through the workplace harmoniously with your coworkers.

WOOD

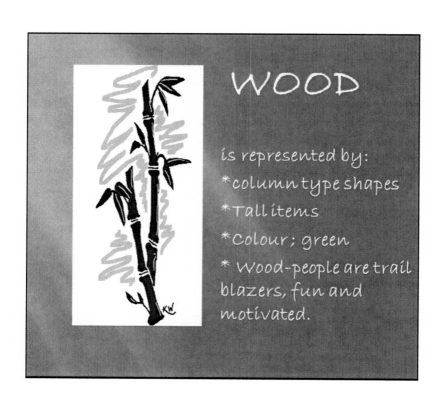

is represented by:
* column type shapes
* Tall items
* Colour; green
* Wood-people are trail blazers, fun and motivated.

Wood People

Wood people are the movers and shakers—the busiest people around! They have great ideas, they have energy, and they have the means to make it happen! Yes! Yes! And, yes, they *do* like to use *lots* of exclamation marks!

If you want the job done, give the task to the busiest person—a person whose dominant element is wood.

The wood element is represented by the season of springtime—a time of growth, high energy and the colour green. There is fresh abundance in the air and new birth of the deciduous trees, flowers, birds and insects. There is newfound energy in the universe. Therefore, wood people will find their task lists growing and their days filled with great ideas and good causes to support.

Wood people tend to be well-balanced, likeable individuals. They are fast learners and have a strong foundation on which to stand in order to succeed. They like to dive in and get things done quickly. They tend to be confident, result-oriented, competitive risk-takers. They love to see a project through to the end, and many become very powerful in their profession.

Common professions for wood people include:

- sales, any and all sectors
- customer service
- real estate
- wedding planner
- entrepreneur
- small business owner
- travel services
- set designer
- advertising/marketing

If you are a wood person, you can enjoy lots of energy, unlimited growth and great rewards working with other wood people. Being an extrovert, you have the ability to easily connect with people, gather them together and work toward a cause.

Many wood people are so good at organizing and delegating, they forget to finish the job—because they are already on to the next one. Other behaviours common to wood people:

- Their desk and office is out of control. They like to see everything, and they like to know where everything is. They prefer to keep things within reach.
- They have a lot of projects on the go. They tend to change the subject quickly and then come back with questions when processing information.
- They often interrupt and like to keep the conversation moving: "Get to the point!"
- Their resting area (personal space) tends to have a plethora of hobbies, books and "things to do" to keep busy.
- They tend to clean up and get rid of things too quickly. A thing needs to have a purpose or it gets moved to the trash. Their motto: "Outta sight, outta mind."

Wood children are often rewarded for being self-starters or natural leaders. While rising to the top of their class, they are often misunderstood by their young friends. Their vocabulary and problem-solving skills can be mature for their age.

As a young child, wood people were probably disciplined for speaking out and standing up for themselves. In fact, they were probably disciplined for being too much of everything—too demanding, too loud, too reckless and too competitive. The irony is that many of these qualities are survival skills they require as adults.

Real Snapshots

The real snapshots following this and subsequent element descriptions are taken from real life. Although the examples are not solely from the workplace, the characteristic behaviours can help you identify these elements, sometimes in their extreme form. The names and some of the professions have been altered to protect each person's identity.

Meg, a wood child full of energy, wanted to experience life to the fullest. She was constantly put down for being too loud and too reckless. She was always the one taken in for stitches as a result of taking risks on the playground. Sifting through her life lessons, she remembers being told to sit down and shut up. She felt her childhood was very stifling.

A busy, fun-loving gal, she had no problem finding work or attracting friends and boyfriends. It is odd that with all these people and acquaintances, she still wasn't fulfilled in life. Meg was always three steps ahead of everybody. Two marriages later, she finally met a guy who can keep up with her, and with this security, she has been able to settle into her career. Meg is still a wood person who has projects on the go constantly.

Donna, a retail salesperson for office services, started out as a part-time employee. She was focused on getting ahead and moved quickly into a supervisor position and then became a regional manager. Never taking the time for a personal life, she excelled in her job performance and received many achievement awards for her successes. Nearing retirement, she was apprehensive about what to do when the time came to slow down. Always ahead of her time, Donna launched a brand-new consulting business on the eve of retirement, wrote a book and is now running training seminars throughout the year—an energetic achievement for anyone and impressive for a lady in her sixties! It is tough to tell a wood person when it is time to stop or slow down.

Joe grew up with a lot of ideas and a lot of energy. I recall Joe as a youngster; he wanted to get out there and travel the world. Too busy to sit still and attend college or university, he jumped from job to job trying to find himself.

When following up with Joe's family, I learned he'd been overseas for a few years. When he first left North America, he drove a huge harvester combine in Australia for one of the farms and then moved on to Southeast Asia to teach English as a Second Language. He is now running his own tour company out of East Asia. (Wood energy—the movers and shakers.)

FIRE

is represented by:
*triangular shapes
*Sharp or bright
objects
*Colour; Red
*Fire-people are
lively, passionate
and energized

Fire People

Fire people are not only on fire, they love the fame that goes with the territory. They crave recognition for being the hero, the one with the great idea or the one who remembered the chocolate cake for the office birthday. They are insightful, full of problem-solving skills and passionate about life.

Fire people like to think outside the box. They like to have fun and have a wide social circle on which to bounce off their ideas. They are understanding, courteous and generally do not hold a grudge. Many are just looking for recognition or fame on a project but don't necessarily need to be the star of the show.

Fire people may also have a reputation for being dramatic and can overreact in any situation at hand. In some cases, they can be rather high-maintenance, consuming other people's time and energy. Fire people are *out there*. While you may only think of celebrities as examples of fire people, there are many right in your own neighbourhood.

Some likely occupations for true fire people:

- actor/actress
- lecturer
- musician
- politician
- preacher
- stand-up comic
- newscaster
- entrepreneur

If you are a fire person, you have energy and passion. You are the one with the social life and seem to have a lot of fun in your life—the more bling, the better. You tend to wear bright colours and are relatively open-minded, with good problem-solving skills.

Someone who is having a "fire moment" while not necessarily being a dominant fire person might frequently speak up to solve problems: "I know where to find one! Everyone should follow me!"

or even "My friend's mom had that same problem and I know all about it." This individual might like to arrive late (on purpose), make an entrance and get attention by interrupting the scene. In other cases, the fire element shows up in the form of anger. The person who has a bad temper or loud behaviour can be extremely disruptive and even violent.

Here are other behaviours common to fire people:

- They like dramatic, bold colour schemes.
- They like to entertain and love the energy that guests bring.
- They will keep their favourite things in sight and show them off: "This is my . . ." and "This is what we picked up in . . . ."
- They can be messy and disorganized, with many unfinished projects on the go.
- Often shopaholics, they like new clothes and shoes. They will dress with the mood of the day and require praise and reinforcement for their choices.
- They seem to be either inspired and passionate or burned out. They may have no way to balance emotions.
- They will display their awards, acknowledgments and pictures with famous people in prominent places, justifying their presence.
- They will often act painfully cheerful, with a motto of "Don't worry, be happy!" or "Look on the bright side of life!"
- They will always have a wild story to tell about their experiences with the dry-cleaner, a hotel, fitness club, etc. They enjoy playing the victim in these situations.
- Many true fire people do not appear to have an off switch, as they give 110 percent daily to the task at hand.

Fire children are often rewarded for making friends easily and brightening people's day with their joyful exuberance. They are happy to be around other people and crave attention for doing well in performing arts—school plays, gymnastics, dancing or singing.

As a young child, fire people were probably disciplined for talking too fast. They are busy people, grabbing the attention from all the other kids. Appearing to be a bit scatterbrained, they can bounce between making light of some situations and providing a dramatic performance in others. Inconsistency with friendships could lead to isolation, which could in turn lead to another dramatic performance.

Real Snapshots

Henry, a corporate executive for a large global company, was in fire mode all the time. He was a polished individual, loved by his family, and he would do just about anything for his four kids. He loved to talk and entertain.

Henry would start by asking about your latest vacation and then proceed to tell you all about *his* vacation. He would try to corner you into a political discussion, and when you decided not to talk politics, he'd tell you about his opinion anyway and how he could solve the worlds' problems.

Don, reassigned from his high-profile (fire person) position in politics, was adjusting to the new environment of having a lesser position. He would wander over to other people's workstations just to chat and offer unsolicited advice. His favourite "catch" was to say something like, "Well, I'm glad *that* is finished!" This would invite someone to inquire "What's finished?" Another favourite of his was, "Have you seen Joe lately? Do you want to know what he's been doing on the 14th floor?" Don, always a nice guy, would be happy to share his knowledge with you about what was going on. After a while, people began to distrust him—too much gossip about other people.

Patrick, a tradesperson in his fifties, decided this was the year to renovate his own home. A perfectionist in his trade, he made sure this house would have the best materials. He forged ahead assembling the best team, purchasing the best copper piping, the best hardwood flooring, the best windows. But there were some results of his obsession to build the best house that he failed to foresee.

It was his wife who went to the bank to finance the renovation. In fact, she had to refinance three times over the next two years in order to continue the process, as Patrick ripped out every wall and stairwell in his master plan to "make it the best." His income suffered as he took more time to work on the house. The wife's income was stable, but they were maxed out on their loan payments and credit cards. They were living in a house under construction for years. No one was happy. Fire people can be driven and consumed in their tasks, so much that they can destroy what they have built.

EARTH

is represented by:
*squares and
rectangles,
*clay, rocks and dirt
*colours; tan, yellow,
caramel, rust, brown
*Earth-people are
warm, honest, loyal
and trust worthy.

Earth People

Earth people are down to earth, trustworthy and sincere. They would give you the shirt off their back if they could, and they are loyal to a fault at times. Earth people are the mediators, the arbitrators and the coordinators of the family and workplace. They are detail-oriented, diplomatic, kind and nurturing. They are the type of employee who likes to please others. They often morph into the role of a trainer for new hires or the go-to for anything in the company. As the nucleus of the family, they are the curators of the information they've collected in order to stay in touch with family, ancestors and high-school chums. Every association and family needs an earth person.

Some likely professions for earth people include:

- nurse
- secretary
- administrative assistant
- customer service
- school teacher
- childcare worker
- pharmacist
- pet-care worker

If you are an earth person, you are seen as a quiet, humble person wearing casual, comfortable clothes. You are reliable, detail-oriented and a great moderator for harmony. You are the one juggling the committee meetings, carpools and PTA meetings. Some earth people burn out because they cannot say no to any and all demands placed on them. Other behaviours common to earth people:

- They like to collect things. Their environment is often cluttered with papers, recipes, books, journals and magazines.

- They always have a full pantry for entertaining anyone who walks in the door. They best connect and nurture others while in the kitchen.
- As collectors of antiques and nostalgia, they love to read memoirs and experience history.
- They like textiles, such as blankets, pillows, tablecloths and draperies. They tend to decorate with small muted patterns and soft colours.
- They have an easygoing personality and cannot say no to those they feel loyal to.
- In extreme cases, they can become meddlesome or manipulative, as they need to be needed. The empty-nest syndrome can be very difficult for these people.
- They can be easily diverted and convinced to go where a need is perceived.
- True peacemakers, they always get into the middle of a confrontation—first to understand the problem and then to keep the peace.
- Comfort is the number-one priority—comfort foods, comfortable beds, comfortable temperatures.

Earth children are often rewarded for being practical when dealing with money and thinking ahead. Their kind and easygoing nature comes with a barrage of questions, trying to understand how the world works. They are mature for their age and make great moms to younger siblings.

As young children, earth people were probably disciplined for sticking their nose in where it didn't belong. They can become shy or sensitive toward the activities they don't understand. Some earth children become quite bossy trying to maintain order on the playground when the group doesn't want to follow the rules of the game.

Real Snapshots

Ellen, a lovely gal in western Canada, is a seamless blend of earth person and metal person. Marrying later in life and having no children of her own, Ellen carved a name out for herself as a teacher of Home Economics. She was precise, inquisitive and a perfectionist, whether baking in the kitchen, sewing or knitting, or tole painting designs on garden furniture.

When she married Ryan, he came with a grown daughter and two grandchildren. Not only did she have the earth-mama role down to a science, but later, she ended up fascinated by genealogy on both sides of the family. Her retirement years are spent head down in papers, writing to extended family, flying off to Utah, compiling memory books and scanning the documents and photos to leave to the next generation. She is so busy and so happy to have this project to do! To see her workspace, you'd think she was running the country. Every pile has a purpose, and she knows *exactly* where everything is. (Typical earth person.)

Ekaterina, a middle-aged Polish lady I met years ago, was a typical stereotype of a Polish earth mama. Although she was a scientist at a research facility, she would always rush home to cook lunch for her grown boys. I asked her, "Ekaterina, your boys are in their twenties. Why do you feel compelled to rush home to cook lunch for them?" And dinner? And more? There was no discussion. If she fed her boys well, they could concentrate on their studies. That was what she wanted to do and what she needed to do.

James is also an earth mama. While this roll is expected in females, many accomplished men also have this as a dominant element. James learned to bake while working at a bakery during his university years. Learning to make pies, buns and bread in the wee hours of the morning was a great job for a student. He still finds cooking and baking to be quite relaxing.

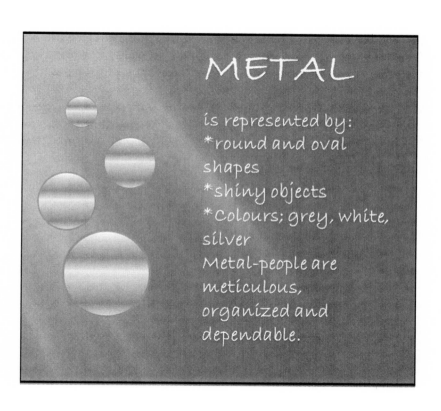

METAL

is represented by:
*round and oval shapes
*shiny objects
*Colours; grey, white, silver
Metal-people are meticulous, organized and dependable.

Metal People

Metal people tend to be a little more introverted than their coworkers. They think in black and white, follow the rules and have an extreme sense of justice. They exhibit precise thinking and are not easily distracted once they get started on a project. They are strong to speak up when someone is bending the rules or trying to instigate a shortcut. They do not fare well with change. They like order, rules and numbers because these are finite and easy to understand. Metal people can be overly analytical and stubborn in situations where they have chosen to stand their ground.

Anywhere that rules and regulations are involved, you'll find a metal person. In work mode, these individuals have a limited sense of humour; they are all business. Some likely professions for metal people:

- doctor
- lawyer
- computer geek/analyst
- bookkeeper
- accountant
- bank teller
- draftsperson
- medical illustrator
- law enforcement
- electrician
- plumber
- engineer
- biologist

If you are a metal person, your shirt will likely be tucked in neatly and the buttons done right up to the neck. You will always present yourself as very organized, composed and professional. A perfectionist with numbers and technology, you will always have the answers.

Another interesting characteristic of metal people is their creative edge. Some develop their skills as fine artists, tradespeople and other jobs that require commitment, accuracy and exactness. Their problem-solving skills show up here with obsessive precision.

Other behaviours common to metal people:

- They can be overly cautious and analytical, as they have trust issues with new concepts and new people.
- They tend to think only with right or wrong answers, which make them hard to deal with in negotiations.
- Introverted and self-sufficient, they work best on projects by themselves.
- They are perfectionists who require a plan that is detail-oriented, organized and feasible.
- Having strong morals and integrity, they will speak up when injustice is suspected.
- They live by the rules and the policy and procedures of the company.
- Their furniture and possessions will be lined up and squared off into neat spaces.
- They will probably not display private-life pictures or knick-knacks at their desk. Their workspace will always be tidy and clean.
- They may express frustration while working with others.

Metal children are often rewarded for acting mature and grown-up. They play independently and keep their bedrooms neat and orderly. These kids are trustworthy and will follow the rules set out for them.

As young children, metal people were probably thought of as being too serious. They didn't have a lot of friends so were often left in their own world with their own odd games and explorations. They could be difficult when adapting to any change in routine or change in the seasons. Metal kids can be picky eaters and most refuse to try something new.

Real Snapshots

Rick, a lawyer, is a typical metal person. He is sceptical and analytical about everything and is indifferent to casual talk. With no need for small talk, he lives with and reacts to whatever he is focusing on that day. Rick is engrossed with his clients, fully dedicated and caring about the impact of the results of their cases. He is focused.

Lily had all the cards lined up for success. She was identified as gifted as a child and therefore encouraged and praised throughout her elementary and high-school years. She went to the local university to study accounting and emerged at the top of her class. This is a good career choice for a metal person.

As time went on, Lily found it more and more difficult to get along with her coworkers. She eventually got fired. She took the company to court for wrongful dismissal and won. This sequence repeated itself several times over the next few years, with Lily always playing the victim and then suing her employer. (Metal with fire-element moments.) She was unable to listen to another point of view, and she was always right.

Caroline was a veteran in her industry, and all its products and procedures were second nature to her. The office manager would send new hires to her for instructions. Caroline's lack of respect for the newbies was apparent by the brash way she spoke to them all. She fumed each day, "I'll do it for you" or "I'm checking to see if you are doing it right."

Caroline's department had a high turnover of employees, as the new hires requested transfers. Caroline was frustrated and finally told Human Resources that whenever she came in to work she felt like she was preparing for a fight. A metal person is not the one to nurture and support new staff members, no matter how much experience he or she may have. Both Caroline and HR should have addressed this years earlier.

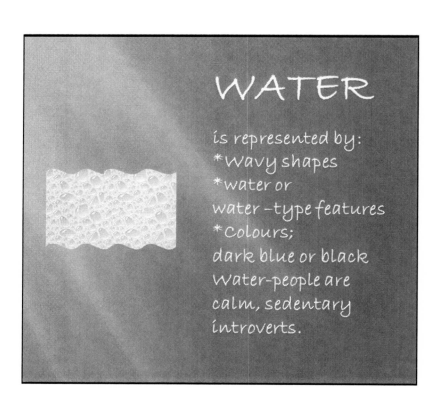

WATER

is represented by:
*wavy shapes
*water or
water–type features
*colours;
dark blue or black
Water-people are
calm, sedentary
introverts.

Water People

Water people can be split into two types: "rushing water" and "deep water." Generally, both types are loners. The first type is rushing around so much, they don't have roots, and the other is so still. For the majority of this section, we'll be examining "deep water."

It is common for senior citizens to shift from a dominant element in their prime to the water element later in life. They have lived their lives and are quieting down, reflecting on the past. Water people have very limited social lives, preferring to experience life through books and documentaries. They are very happy in their position as armchair travellers. If you compare this to sitting in deep water, true water people can actually become stuck in their lives and even be depressed. They need to think and plan out everything in advance: where to go, where to park and who is going to be there. It takes a lot of effort to change the mind of "deep water" people, let alone get them moving.

Water people are very well read and generally succeed in a profession that deals with specific precision, similar to metal people. Their sense of humour can be distorted, almost dry and cunning. They are hoping to impress you with their wit and know-how, sometimes doing a lot more harm than good. It is common for people to grow into this element as their career matures and they are able to provide calm, wise counsel or service in their chosen profession.

Common professions for water people include:

- judge
- surgeon
- banker/lender
- philosopher
- author
- physicist

If you are a "deep water" person, you can be identified by some of the phrases you use every day: "I can't do that" or even "You can't do that!" This likely means you haven't taken the time to think through that (inconceivable) idea . . . yet. You take pride in thinking things through. Prematurely, you often challenge simple ideas, treating them like something barbaric or catastrophic.

Water people generally do not have a faith. As deep thinkers and very private individuals, they have already figured out where they stand in the universe. Their expert knowledge will support this view.

Other behaviours common to "deep water" people:

- They can be introverted. They prefer that other people put out the effort to communicate or bring them information. Depression is common.
- They believe they are busy all the time, when actually they have a set routine and are not willing to alter it to accommodate others.
- They can be stingy and critical of others' spending, morals and choices.
- They will have original, imaginative ideas and then lean on others to execute them.
- They are very observant and well-read—seekers of the truth.
- They like to work and live in sparsely furnished surroundings.
- They contemplate their place in the big picture of life.
- They can have difficulty with conformity, changing routine, moving offices or reshuffling the team. They could be stubborn and then retreat (not happily) when pushed into certain situations.
- They like living near the water or, failing that, displaying art with water features.
- They like their creature comforts: a high-end mattress, a big TV, a nice easy chair.

Water children are often rewarded for being observant and able to think through problems for themselves. Their imagination and creativity show up through their writing and essays at school, confirming that they are very smart kids.

As a young child, water people were probably disciplined for being blunt and tactless—putting others down with insults. They can be very sceptical of their surroundings, and they trust no one to enter their secretive world. This leads to suspicion and a nonconformist attitude toward the games the other children play. I have only met a few water children. These kids with their sober moods appear to be little adults rather than children. Survival for water people in childhood probably means imaginary friends and living the life of a loner.

Real Snapshots

Rob, a "deep water" person, was an English gentleman. His wife died a few years before I met him and his adult children were all off leading their own lives. Long retired, he had only himself to look after.

For his 79th birthday, he bought himself a huge 48-inch flat-screen TV and a new La-Z Boy chair. Later, he added on to his cable bundle in order to watch the "scream channel." Why the "scream channel"? Because he thought it was funny! Rob had all he needed in his life. He wasn't going anywhere, and no one could convince him otherwise.

Sue is a lady in her mid-fifties. Her frustrated relationship with her lawyer mom has consumed her entire adult life. Her mother was unappreciative of her accomplishments and was generally focused on her cases when Sue was around. Sue worked many years as a secretary and catered to other people's needs (earth qualities). She married a fellow more than 10 years older than herself. They did not have any children.

Sue has been more contemplative with her life as she approaches 60 years old. Lately, she has turned into a deep water person. She cries a lot, is depressed most days and drinks a bit too much every day to cope. She seems to be stuck lingering in the past rather than seeing the great life she has now or could have in the future. Sue doesn't have the motivation to get back to work. She'll likely need counselling or therapy if she can't shake this herself. As stated earlier, it is really tough to move water people when they are stuck.

Ray was the youngest of seven children. His mom worked outside the home and his dad was a hardworking labourer. Ray was basically raised by his siblings—three older brothers and three older sisters. Without a lot of supervision in the house, Ray witnessed amazing screaming fights between his sisters and fistfights between his brothers. He confided that he often felt he was sitting on the windowsill looking in at a movie. Always the observer, he never learned to trust anyone completely.

Ray fell into being a water person purely as a tactic for his own survival. An accomplished electrician by day and a musician at night, Ray wrapped himself up with rules and societal norms to fit in. Definitely a loner, he resisted growth and development in himself. Any change in work schedules, technology or routine sends him into a depression.

Larry has moved through most of the five-element cycle in his life. He spent his early years moving from country to country with his family in an executive lifestyle. He was well-read, came from a supportive loving family and had grand ideas for forging ahead in his life. Larry was convinced he could get rich on his own life experiences and didn't need formal education (wood).

He spent the early years overriding people's opinions and authority (fire) and stepping on a few of toes along the way. He married the "girl," had the "kid," bought the "house" and did everything that society told him he should. Yet Larry never really figured out how to fit into society (metal).

After a few decades, he ended up on the beach selling ice cream, convinced that he had "beat the system." He could collect a welfare check and still get paid to sell ice cream (wood, again). Larry finally gave up, hit rock bottom and received psychiatric help. He now spends his time trying to solve the world's problems from his little apartment, cynical and resentful for his lack of success (deep water).

In My Element

I'd like for people to think I'm a well-rounded element. The truth is that I am a dominant wood person. I was trying to refrain from being labelled, but it is really tough to hide a wood personality. I naturally venture into the fire-element zone, and I do retreat into the cool water element when needed. (The next chapter refers to the element cycles.)

More than 15 years ago, I married an earth person. One thing we like to do together is go sailing. For me, the calmness of the water is relaxing. For Stephen, when he goes into racing mode, he morphs into a metal person. He loves to fuss on his boat: all the details, the trimmings, the technical data he uses to go faster, be better, and go farther. A good finish in a race is his triumph for the day. Same sport, different agenda.

In the next chapters, I'll show how the elements are arranged in cycles and how you can use these to find support in the other elements—very practical when choosing a partner for life or for work.

~~~

Wood people and fire people are both outgoing people.
And although they get along,
they often seek out quieter individuals for a partnership.

~~~

CHAPTER 5

Using the Elements to Understand People

Now that you know your element and those of the people around you, we can begin to explore how to use this knowledge. In any business or personal relationship, once you have figured out how to talk with people and it works, life is so much better.

Elemental Communications

For successful business communications with *wood people*:

- Firmly establish your credibility. Focus on results and get right down to business.
- Make eye contact. Wood people are a loyal, sincere group and don't have time to deal with someone they are trying to figure out.
- Keep the pace moving when presenting ideas, as wood people are fast thinkers and can be way ahead of you.
- Watch for frustration—that means that you missed something. Either your facts are not lined up or you are glossing over something obvious.
- Don't cheat. Once your credibility is compromised, they will not support you.
- Wood people like options. When closing a deal, give them an either-or choice so they still feel they are in control.

When dealing with a superior, you can still offer a choice: "Would you like that report on your desk before lunch or after lunch?"

For successful business communications with *fire people*:

- Keep things light and fun to get their attention. They like to talk about themselves.
- Praise them and thank them for their ideas and input.
- They'll lose attention quickly if you ask too much from them in an area in which they cannot excel. And yet, they may come up with great ideas. Listen carefully.
- Proposals and solutions should be exciting and dramatic. Use colour!
- If they are getting off the topic, give them a few minutes to talk it out before bringing the conversation back to the issue at hand.
- Always follow up. They like to know that you are behind them. Be a fan.
- Do not upset them. They have loose loyalties and will (perhaps bluntly) move along.
- Hugs are okay—when initiated by them.

For successful business communications with *earth people*:

- Make them comfortable. Offer tea, coffee or water and sit together to make a connection.
- Gentle small talk is a good start. Ask earth people about their family and what types of things they do on the weekends.
- Don't rush an earth person. Leave time to ask questions, process and ask more questions.
- Listen carefully. An earth person will tell you exactly what he or she wants to hear.
- Offer simple solutions to solve problems. *Practical, down-to-earth, recyclable, eco-friendly* and *natural* are

good buzzwords. Earth people like to think they are doing a good deed with their choices.

- Their main goal is "Don't rock the boat!" They want to see how everyone involved will be affected before acting.
- Hugs are okay after you've developed a firm and mutual connection.

For successful business communications with *metal people*:

- Respect the boundaries they have set. Sit where they want you to sit and leave when they want you to leave.
- Be professional and do not interrupt a metal person.
- Metal people need you to notice the detail they have put into the project and the time that went into the presentation. Just notice; do not be excessive in your praise.
- Follow the rules and the procedures metal people lay out initially. These guidelines have been well thought out and could work, so give them a try.
- When dividing tasks, find an extrovert (wood or fire) to do the public and social tasks, leaving the metal person to do the quieter ones. Everyone will be a winner.
- Make a checklist and duplicate it so that everyone knows what each person is doing. For the metal person, this is a form of rules and provides needed guidelines.
- Do not ever try to hug a metal person without permission.

For successful business communications with *water people*:

- Develop a rapport and trust over time.
- Give them time to think, process and digest the information before asking for an endorsement. Water people analyse things in a deep way.
- Slow down your speech when presenting new ideas. Breathe. Make sure each point gets enough consideration. Be creative and original.

- Water people like to know the big picture. Be a visionary when trying to make a point. Watch for cynical barbs and criticism; they are really asking questions.
- Develop a support network. Water people need help from others to make their dreams a reality.
- Listen for the use of a cynical tone, such as "What would you want to do *that* for?" This tone makes any discussion fall flat. The tone could actually mean, "I'm not interested" or "Don't try to convince me."
- Do not even *try* to encourage a water person to stand in the limelight.

Where to Tread Lightly

Wood People

In most cases, wood people pull up their socks and bounce back from adversity. They are survivors, and they have ideas and the energy to carry on. But as with all the elements, there are some things to watch out for.

A wood person's worst fear can be summed up as loss of power. As survivors, their whole philosophy of being in control is their *life*. Any circumstance that involves powerlessness, helplessness or being confined to quarters is detrimental. They need space in order to gather ideas and keep the momentum. They are the first to grab the ball or a new idea and run with it. When the road is blocked or they are confused and beaten down, they don't have anywhere to grow. With loss of power and no vision, they will move on—"I'm outta here!"

Fire People

A fire person's worst fear is being cut off from an audience. A timeout, a pink slip or a layoff can lead to disaster. This derailment in a fire person's world will lead to inactivity, separation, confusion and isolation. If you intentionally upset their world, fire people will seek retaliation. They need people and will seek out approval from another source if they don't get it in their present situation.

Fire people need to learn how to control their spontaneous energy, as their antics can be very distracting to coworkers. Finding an after-hours outlet for free expression could be helpful to balance their energy in the workplace. Fire people need to recognize that most individuals they deal with cannot function with the same vitality. The wood element can help. Teaming up with wood people or making use of wood objects can help them manage their projects and commitments.

Earth People

An earth person's worst fear would be to feel unimportant or not needed. Earth people thrive on fussing over their charges, whether a department team at work or the family unit at home. This is their security. They do not work well independently or enjoy the limelight. The last thing you want to do to is leave earth people alone or separate them from the fold.

Earth people may need to develop more self-esteem and learn to say no. When they are overextended, earth people will no longer feel fulfilled tending to the ones depending on them. They may need to connect with some fire elements. Fire objects and things that are red often promote optimism and enthusiasm in earth people.

Metal People

One of a metal person's worst fears is a world without rules and guidelines. Metal people spend so much of their lives learning to do what is right socially, politically and morally that they are often worried they could lose control if they try to experience spontaneity or intimacy. They are stressed trying to keep everything on track. At times, even a small change could cause a meltdown.

Metal people need social involvement. Perhaps they could schedule time for different activities outside of work hours. Given a few choices, they may figure out how they can become a little less uptight and more sociable. Warm characteristics and qualities that are present in the earth element can help to relax and stabilize a metal person's extreme life. A metal person who prefers to stay a loner will need to find an outlet to satisfy the need for mental stimulation.

Water People

A water person's main fear would be vulnerability. Water people do not want their privacy invaded. They are very possessive of their ideas, research and accomplishments, and they do not want their identity misrepresented or stolen. Having little or no faith to rely on, they can be extremely pessimistic.

"Rushing water" people are a little different. They can feel trapped, depressed and unorganized while being overextended at the same time. They may still keep pushing themselves without a solid plan until they become road blocked. Think of a kayak going down the rapids and hitting a sandbar.

I see "rushing water" people as fallen, depressed wood people trying to get back on track. Referring back to wood-people and their traits, the optimism, the planning and the energy are all there. What is missing is the organization, the attention to details and the delegation. "Rushing water" people are the ones you see breathlessly running in for meetings, unprepared and ruffled. They spend their time putting out fires and setting new ones. They are too busy, always on the edge of a burnout, and they can't seem to organize their time or their tasks. Stuck in endless activity, they're getting nowhere.

Water people need to soften their tough exterior. They really need the help of the other four elements to be well-balanced individuals. If a water person could find a soft spot for a spouse or loved one, this could be a great starting point for adding warmth, trust and balance. Another thing water people need is the structure and boundaries enforced through metal-element qualities. More mental stimulation could help them get back on track.

Reader Challenge

Have a look around your desk and key areas. Is your dominant element represented in anyway? Is it time to reinforce your goals in life with more visuals and support from the elements?

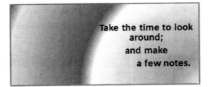

Take the time to look
around;
and make
a few notes.

~~~

Knowing our own dominant element is not enough; we need to experience our other elements, not only to become well rounded, but to further understand our coworkers, clients and family.

When I was 26, with a few successes under my belt, I enquired about moving up in the company. My supervisor flat out told me I was too young. Too young—isn't that discrimination? But after further discussion and contemplation on my part, I understood. As we mature into our element, there is the opportunity to grow through the other elements to become a better, well-rounded person.

This takes time.

~~~

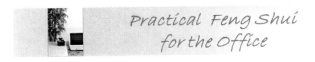

CHAPTER 6

Circling the Elements

The five elements are arranged in a specific sequence in a circle, as shown in the next few diagrams. The arrangement of the five elements shows how they can interact, and this can be used in feng shui to balance the strength of tangible objects. A quick look at fire, for example, reveals:

- Earth suppresses fire. If there is a predominance of red in a room (fire), it can be balanced by adding an earth element.
- Wood feeds fire. If the room has a weak fire element, the fire can be amplified by adding a wood element.
- Water extinguishes fire. Too much of the water element can smother the fire properties in a room.

The example above shows three possible interactions for only one element, fire. To expand on this for all the elements, think of these interactions as cycles within the circle of the five elements. A feng shui consultant will work with these elemental cycles when trying to find balance in a room or building.

Rather than focusing on tangibles in this chapter, we will focus on using these cycles to find the balance between the elements associated with different personalities. The results are fascinating! There are three cycles I'll discuss: productivity and growth cycle, a rest and recovery cycle and a cycle of aggressive behaviour. Each cycle shows a different way the five elements interact, and this can be the key for you to understand your relationships with other people. While flourishing in your key personal element, you can use the first two cycles to seek support from elements on either side—to grow or to rest. The third cycle deals with your opposite element. Reflections on your personal growth and life experiences will help you further understand the movements of the different cycles.

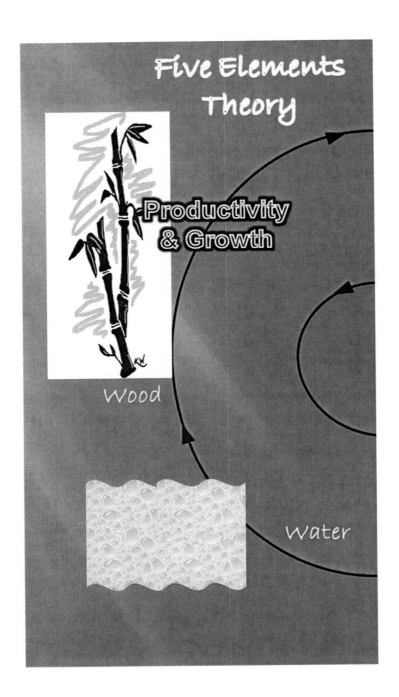

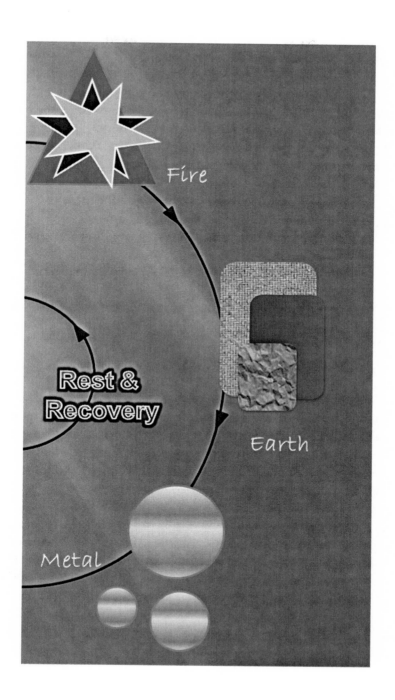

Fire

Earth

Rest & Recovery

Metal

The Productivity and Growth Cycle

This first cycle shows how you can cultivate your potential with support from your adjacent element, clockwise in the circle. I find this cycle fascinating as well as extremely practical. The productivity and growth cycle is just that: productive, progressive and nurturing. This is how one element helps another.

- Water nourishes wood (allowing wood to grow).
- Wood feeds the fire (so fire can consume).
- Fire burns out and forms earth (giving earth a foundation).
- Earth (in time) creates metal (giving metal rigidity and strength).
- Metal contains or moves water (giving water focus and purpose).

This cycle becomes an endless loop.

Smooth associations with people and your environment can change from year to year, season to season, month to month, circumstance to circumstance, person to person. Just as native flora can adapt to different regions, we all need to adapt to our specific surroundings from one work environment to another. To be well-rounded, we need to get along with everyone.

How we live out our lives may shift again and again as we change and grow. A solid relationship in our twenties grows and changes as we move into our thirties, fifties and beyond. We simply adjust and adapt to each new environment, gathering new information and learning new skills along the way. This is the art of balance. Change, as we grow, is inevitable.

The Rest and Recovery Cycle

[Note: In BTB, this cycle is generally referred to as the *reducing cycle*: one element can reduce the effect of the element situated counter clockwise in the cycle. When applying this cycle to people and personalities rather than objects, I prefer to use rest and recovery, as I believe this cycle can be adapted as a means to regroup from the stressors in your day and balance the elements that are weak.]

This section helps you identify the need for rest and recovery. There will always be a to-do list waiting for you. I really hope that you can take some of the suggestions in this section to heart. I believe that when you embrace your key personal element, the element cycles can help you function through life's adventures.

Burnout and exhaustion are inevitable in today's work scene, no matter how we define it. We all react differently to life's stressors. Try to recognize when you need a break or a timeout and be kind to yourself. Functioning in your element is fabulous, but you will need a recharging period between peak performances. Rest and recovery are important. People can have different concerns and different setbacks in different situations. We need to learn to adapt. For example, a promotion can lead to another level of politics and challenges that create another level of growth and stress.

Here's how I interpret the rest and recovery cycle:

- Wood revitalizes through water. (Wood is nourished when it rests in water.)
- Water recharges through metal. (Water becomes charged through metal conductivity.)
- Metal converts to earth. (Metal can set aside harshness and experience the softness of earth.)
- Earth regenerates through fire. (Earth revives with fire.)
- Fire regulates though wood (Fire can refuel with wood energy resources).

Each element experiences burnout a bit differently and has a different way of recovering. For example, *wood people*, as busy and organized as they are, can have their fire moments and step up to the plate. But remember, fire can be consuming to wood people. They can burn out easily. In fact, burnout is always pending for true wood people. When fatigue and despair settle in, wood people need to get out of the fire, and then retreat. The best way for wood people to retreat is to get deep into the water element to pacify the soul. The water is not only cooler than the fire; it is a place where the wood people can be nourished. Wearing cool colours can also be calming and aid in recovery.

Fire people will burn out a little differently than wood people. They tend to consume the energy of those around them and leave the ashes to fall where they may. After reading about fire people earlier in this book, you may recognize people having a fire moment or a wood moment without necessarily being dominant in either element. Fire people ask wood people to participate in their projects because they need the wood energy to keep going. When fire people tire and need to refuel, it is important for them to self-regulate within the wood element. This still gives them the satisfaction of participation, attention and team energy, but not the spotlight. When they have refuelled, they can regroup and get back onstage.

When *earth people* burn out, they tend to be discreet, unobtrusive and quiet. Generally, the will to keep things the same is both important and stressful for earth people. They avoid change. Being overwhelmed with details can cause them to work harder, and they can easily start behaving like metal people—rigid, precise and uncompromising. By trying to get things right and fix things, they will perpetuate more work. A fix for earth people who are overcommitted and underappreciated could be to step back and retreat into fire elements. Earth people are drawn to fire people's projects when they need to let someone else take the lead. By regenerating through the fire energy, earth people can set aside their self-appointed deadlines and task lists, lighten up, share a few jokes and take time to relish the moment.

Metal people are tough ones to read, as they will not allow their emotions to show. They tend to burn out when someone or something has upset their world, such as disorder, fraud and misconduct. Intolerant of any of these issues, they will be burnt out by anxiety. Being unable to sleep or to talk about moral issues can send them into a tailspin. Metal people who are rallying for a cause need to know when they need support. If they can't get people to listen, their own anxiety could induce an ulcer. A step back into earth-element qualities can be a quiet and comforting break from the rules and regulations of metal world. The earth approach can help them think clearly. Observing the situation from the sidelines inspires a new strategy to continue. Metal people should consider partaking in a few creature comforts—sip hot apple cider or watch a movie for a change. After taking the time to calm down a bit, they may see how they can redirect their energies.

Quiet and very private, *water people* will never tell you that they are burned out. They are afraid of being exposed. They enjoy being left alone, yet dread being abandoned. A water person who may appear to remain in control, even during something major such as a political or corporate scandal, may actually be totally stressed out. When faced with burnout, water people must seek support to ward off depression. They can find solace and recharge with the qualities and quiet organized space of the metal element. Completing crossword puzzles, playing cards or finding other mental distractions will keep a water person's mind occupied. Water people need to secure a support group that they can trust as they look ahead and ask about alternative solutions to rectify the situation.

Let's face facts—regardless of your element, when you are stressed out, you cannot be productive. Take the time to notice when you are stressed and try to identify the problem. Then take steps to manage it before you accelerate out of control.

Reader Challenge

Take note of the last time you were overwhelmed working on a project. How did you handle yourself? The situation? Did you manage to fit in some recovery methods? Can you see a pattern forming? A productive pattern? Room for improvement? What are you going to do differently the next time?

Problem identification can lead to a solution. Just recently, I hired a virtual assistant. She can sort out the social media—marketing, the mailing lists and whatever else I need. Her swiftness and expertise in this area is amazing. Right now, working very part-time, she has freed up all kinds of time for me to focus on other projects.

> This is a good place to take a break
> before moving to the
> Aggressive Cycle in the next section.

~~~

While water and fire are complete opposites, these elements need each other to help maintain control. Water will always represent the force that stores, accumulates and restores after release. Fire will always symbolize the end point of expansion and consummation of fuel and energy.

~~~

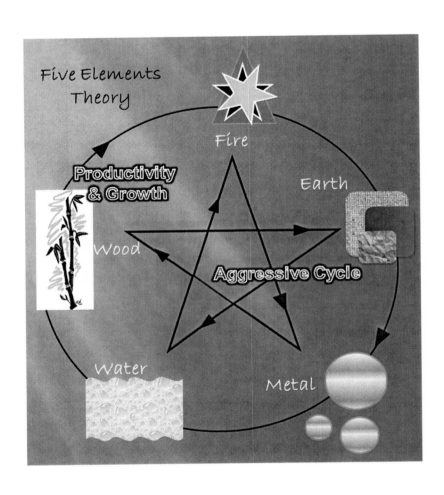

The Cycle of Aggressive Behaviour

[Note: This cycle is often referred to as the *destructive cycle* or the *restraining cycle* when used by feng shui consultants in balancing tangible elements in an environment. The sharp points of the star between these elements can be destructive and penetrating. By using the term *aggressive behaviour* for personality associations, I wish for you to observe behaviour between the elements without thinking about your peers as destructive. We can find solutions for dealing with different types of people—we can all learn to get along.]

We've seen how adjacent elements can nurture you to greater productivity and aid with rest and recovery. This third cycle looks at the opposite elements. These are defined by drawing a star pattern across the circle of the five elements. Those on opposite sides in this cycle can have a detrimental influence on each other, but we still need them. The real challenge is finding a way to work within these parameters.

Our coworkers and members of our teams can all have the same goal, yet find different ways to achieve it. When we get out of our individual cubicle, we can sometimes rub people the wrong way (and vice versa). When teams start to get stressed, more things start to go wrong and the cycle of aggressive behaviour can be set in motion. Sometimes people just can't see eye to eye. Identify with the representations in this cycle:

- Wood element disrupts earth. (Trees can break through the ground.)
- Earth element dams water. (Earth can actually redirect water.)
- Water element extinguishes fire. (Enough water can drown a fire)
- Fire element melts metal. (Enough fire can re-form metal.)
- Metal element cuts wood. (Sharp metal can chop down trees.)

Take a moment to ponder this cycle. These are aggressive words—appropriate when referenced with the sharp, pointed shape of the star. Let's look at the ways aggression makes its way around the cycle, for each of the elements.

Wood: It is possible for a wood person to devour an earth person. A wood person's aggressive words and over-enthusiasm can overwhelm a calm earth person. The wood person can choose to remain calm when dealing with sensitive earth people, but it is often tough to hold back the excitement, particularly when wood is motivated to go-go-go!

Earth: Though kind-hearted, earth people can stifle water people. As earth dams up water, it is possible for earth people to confine the movements of water people. Too much coaxing and too much smothering can totally detach and freeze the water person. Be thoughtful, but know when it is best to leave the water person alone. Your co-worker does not want to join in or go to lunch; water people actually *do* accomplish their best work alone.

Water: Knowing that water people are the quietest, it is a bit odd that their favourite target is fire people. In reality, it is easy to understand, because fire people are out there performing and vulnerable. The sting of a water person can literally put out or drown a fire person. It could be a bad review, a mocking tone or a sly sense of humour that humiliates the fame-seeker. Water people need to be aware their humour can be cutting and not funny at all.

Fire: For fire people, it is all about *"Me!"* They can melt down the metal people in Accounting with ease, maybe just for the fun and excitement. Fire people may get an adrenaline surge when being a bully, but it will be short-lived. They cannot refuel by hanging out with metal people.

Metal: Metal people get tied up in knots when things don't go their way. Their targets are usually wood people because they are the risk-takers. Yes, metal chops wood, and their words are cutting tools. Wood people do require more maintenance in order to, for example, get them to finish their reports. If you want anything completed ahead of time, you may have to—wait for it—*compromise!* Wood people are the ones blazing the trail across the planet, and they have a lot of projects. They will get the job done but not necessarily when you want it.

Want to neutralize all that aggression? Here are some strategies to try.

- *If you are a wood person,* remember that it is the metal person's job to enforce the rules, keep the books and keep track of everyone and their receipts. Details, details, details. Identify this source of friction between the two of you and then try to cooperate and keep your commitments.
- *If you are an earth person* on the receiving end of a wood person's aggression, offer to support the project or event but otherwise steer clear. You will not be able to keep up with wood people. Be aware that you are only opening yourself up for more criticism, as you cannot do the job fast enough, big enough or strong enough.
- *If you are a water person,* you are dealing with earth people's baggage. They are playing the mother figure, and you are on their mind. "You should come and join us!" they'll say. A polite answer is the best way to handle these requests. Then continue to do what you need to do. No stress and no need to worry.
- *If you are a fire person* and having a bad day, just try to stay away from water people. Seriously.
- *If you are a metal person,* look out for your nemesis, the fire person. An overabundance of a fire element in your corner can lead to a meltdown. Let fire people enjoy their fame while it lasts; no need to participate. Now you know that fire people are all about consumption, keep your head up!

The cycle of aggressive behaviour does exist, although it is often denied. This topic always manages to provoke lively discussions. If you refer back to the chart, you can see that your element can appear to be a bully to another element while a third element bullies you. I know, because I've been there. I've been accused of being a bully (What?), and I've been on the receiving end of a bully (Really?). It is not always possible to have control of the entire office and all its interactions. Business needs do come first, sometimes at the risk of bruised egos. Be aware of the effects of your actions on other people.

CHAPTER 7

Assemble Your Team

When evaluating the impact of stressors on a project, the same intensity level can be exhilarating to a wood person, devastating to an earth person and paralyzing to a water person.

~~~

Just as you choose your friends and activities, it is important to choose your team selectively. You will need different people to fulfil the Sales team, the Marketing team, Accounting, Media, Maintenance, etc. Just because their education or background specifies one thing or another, the bigger question should be: Are they a good fit?

As you learn the patterns of which elements you best get along with, also pay attention to the people on the opposite side of the cycle of aggressive behaviour. They are the ones with a uniquely different set of skills. We need diversity on our teams to create balance, to foster discussions of new ideas and to delegate various tasks. Recall the dynamics mentioned in the previous chapter.

When assembling a team, be sure to include diverse personalities. You'll need wood people for the ideas and the insight, fire people for energy, earth people to supply harmony and a grounded opinion, metal people for accountability and water people to give you approval for allowing change to happen.

Team Goals

Your team members need to develop clear goals and coordinate with each other. Without this initial exercise, someone can and will veer off on a tangent without noticing, setting back deadlines and wasting funds. Again, be clear about the goals and make them prominent. I've seen some fabulous visuals in offices informing everyone how many boreholes they've dug so far, how many T-shirts have been sold, how much more work there is to do for the fundraiser. The more visuals, confirmations and information you display to reinforce team goals, the more everyone is onboard, moving and working together. Give your team the tools they need to succeed!

~~~

If you are trying to score in a basketball game
without a basket,
all you are really doing is dribbling.

~~~

A boost in your department could be initiated by sending your team for training and professional development. It can be difficult to measure the benefits right away, but it is extremely important for people to network and learn new skills.

Ask that they all report back after attending a workshop or seminar, just so you can measure their participation and productivity. In feng shui, this is the time to take advantage of the fresh ch'i that has entered into the office. Set new goals, rearrange the cubicles and turn the page for a new project. Relate this to coming back from vacation: You are motivated, rested and have new information to process. No need to settle back into your old routines. Apply what you have learned at the seminar and start moving.

In other instances, a short-term boost in sales or a new contract could allow you to bring in new people. New people bring in new energy, fresh ideas and new dynamics. In fact, the expense of bringing in new staff or paying for a morale boost shows that you care about your team, and your team will respond accordingly.

In order to make a change in your department or your life, something has to shift. Sometimes, it is as easy as removing an obstruction, changing an attitude and setting very clear goals. The new ch'i energy in the workplace has a domino effect and will be noticed by neighbouring teams and clients.

~~~

On one side we have the extroverts, wood people
and fire people. They are both social beings and enjoy
the excitement in the world. Metal people and water
people are the introverts. They are the ones who
follow the rules and hold up moral values in society.
And then we have earth people who are in the middle,
and they like it that way! The earth people are the
neutral force insisting that everyone get along.

~~~

Utilize Your People for Success

Utilize your people to the best of their abilities. You should know who you can call in a pinch to troubleshoot a problem and who has related skills to handle any emergencies. Don't forget about other transferable assets that include creativity, people skills, first-aid experience and foreign-language fluency. What you shouldn't do is ask your Controller to make a Web page for your new product. He may be good with computers, but this does not guarantee you will get the Web page you want.

I worked in one facility that chose to trim the overhead budget a bit by letting go the cleaning staff. We were all responsible for cleaning our own office and for pitching in once a week to vacuum the lobby, clean the toilets and empty the trash. I don't really need to give you details about how this turned out—let's just say some people's standards of *clean* were very different from others'. When I greeted one client in a less-than-acceptable lobby, I decided that I had to take over this task myself or risk ruining my reputation. I waited for this situation to run its course; eventually, sanity prevailed, and management rehired the cleaning staff.

In this case, the team wasn't willing to take the cleaning seriously, as the priority was the sales quota. The management needed to hire professional cleaners. Consider an agency to source out extra help whenever help is needed.

Questions to Consider When Hiring New Salespeople

Your salespeople need to have wood-element or fire-element skills—the extroverts. As well as personal success stories, they will need to have qualities of accountability (metal or earth elements). They will also need to be able to work both independently and as a team. How will you evaluate these traits? Do you need a team leader?

Are your current salespeople too similar to each other? Are they all going after the same target? Do you need people who are more diverse and can cover new territories and areas?

Questions to Consider When Hiring New Technicians or Lab Personnel

Your technicians will require metal element or water element characteristics—the introverts. They need to work independently and need to be precise and trustworthy. How will you evaluate this experience? Are they organized? Their research will need to be completed by a deadline and then submitted. Also, are they trained to write a good report?

Are you looking for new ideas for the project? Do you require fresh concepts to get the results you are looking for? If so, you'll need to look for some wood-element qualities in your new person to add to the team.

Reader Challenge

Record which skills and qualities you require from each team member. When rearranging, assembling or evaluating your current team, this list will help you in choosing replacements when and if required.

~~~

If we learn to choose our teams properly,
we can all reap the rewards together without stress, anger and
anxiety.

~~~

Assimilation

Problems with dynamics can arise in situations where there are new people merging into your team, whether due to reorganization, downsizing or even a positive move to a new location. Some team members could feel threatened, thinking that they are all in competition with each other. Dividing your teams into smaller groups with definite goals can help the transition. Smaller groups provide more opportunities to ask questions and feel included, rather than being anonymous in larger groups.

It takes time to get new teams to gel. To assimilate into an existing group, new people will need to know the routine and expectations and perhaps ingest a huge amount of background material before they can actually start working. Some companies have a go-to person assigned to new employees. Make a point to check in with the new arrivals regularly, depending on the job, to see if any clarification is required. Keep them informed of the longer-term corporate goals and the bigger picture as well as the smaller day-to-day events.

Make sure you are clear with your expectations if you plan to update or add more new people to the project. The time spent in the early stages is crucial for forming a strong foundation—not only rules and regulations but also trust, integrity and values—that brings people together to meet the goals.

The Pyramid

So you have chosen a well-functioning team, but to be most effective, your team needs to be properly assembled within the corporate framework. To find out why the best-run offices run smoothly, you always start at the top with the CEO. He or she must delegate fairly, respect the entire staff, support the projects that staff members are working on and clearly communicate the corporate vision. The next level of management can then follow this lead, to the next level, and so on, and so on.

CEO
Vice-Pres.
General Managers
Dept. Managers, Project Staff
Support Staff, Mail Room & Delivery

Feng shui will give you the tools to understand your people and take control of your environment. This renewed energy will infiltrate through your entire surroundings. It is practical, common sense.

CHAPTER 8

Finding the Wealth

Wealth, in terms of feng shui, speaks of luck, fortune and abundance. These won't materialize without some sort of effort on our part; fortunes don't fall out of the sky very often. We need to define what we are seeking in order to find what we are looking for. Luck, fortune and abundance can be found in many forms.

When people ask me about wealth and abundance, I turn the question back to them: What do you mean by wealth? What are you looking for? Abundance can show up in the form of many grandchildren, magnificent flowers or a litter of kittens. Wealth can be measured in acquisitions—a strong portfolio, real estate and bank accounts. It also shows up in the process of finding the right, affordable home. It is figuring out where to invest your time and money. It takes an effort to search for the strongest financial instrument to secure your future.

How we deal with money and wealth can usually be traced back to the attitudes formed by our parents and their approach to money. We need to look at our barriers, restrictions and fears, often instilled by others. These barriers determine our self-worth, and overcoming them is the key to our success and earnings. When we deal with the real issues and look at things differently, we can open up new definitions of what wealth means to us. From there, we can each define our goals properly.

Success can be measured by achieving goals and then experiencing the rewards. You could be saving up for that long-awaited vacation and then search for sale prices to make your special purchase. It is being optimistic. It is all about looking forward and finding the opportunities that are out there.

~~~

Each of us is a millionaire.
It is hidden beneath years of programming from our parents,
our ancestors and our society at large.
—Sonia Haynes, *The Power of Money*

~~~

The first step is to adjust the energy around you and make changes. Clean your space and clear out the clutter. The action of cleaning is such a simple and practical way for you to take control of your wealth area. You should handle each item yourself and select which things you want to use in your fresh new space. If you do plan to keep a few things, clean and reorganize with good intentions to keep this place special. Each room—whether it be your office, the dining room or the bedroom—will come with its own challenges to find what fits.

Chinese culture uses passionate adjectives when talking about wealth. Words like *lucky, good fortune, auspicious, promising* and *favourable* are often used in decisive reasoning. In most cases, they place an enhancement in the areas where they desire opportunities and reinforcements.

Enhancements

Think of enhancements as attention-getters. Feng shui has an assortment of choices that can bring attention to your space.

- *Lights:* Good lighting, mirrors and light-refracting objects gather energy and move it around. Crystal balls, vases or jewellery work well too. Place your mirrors where they can bring in more light and reflect something pleasant to look at.

- *Sounds:* Softer, pleasant sounds are far better for concentration and productivity. White noise can block out unwanted distractions, or you could try wind chimes or bells. Hung near an entrance, chimes can announce a customer or, alternately, an intruder.
- *Colours:* Choose items that are bright-coloured—neon orange, purple and red. The intention could be to attract attention toward a product, your business achievements or yourself.
- *Life:* Plants that are blooming, have berries or are red in colour are great enhancements. They don't even need to be real—you can bring in a quality representation of a plant for your enhancement. Any bonsai, bright flowers or fish that you choose, real or man-made, are great enhancements.
- *Children and Pets:* The life energy that these beings bring, as exhausting as they may be, do enhance our lives. Pictures of loved ones are fine to bring into the office.
- *Moving Objects:* Wind-powered or electrically powered mobiles or whirligigs can also be classed as enhancements. They stimulate circulation in a stale area. Any movement can awaken the monotony of long corridors.
- *Heavy Objects:* A heavy stone or statue, when properly placed, can help you stay grounded. If you are trying to secure a project, deal with a situation or just be more focused, a rock can stabilize the situation.

Take a look at your space. Count up the enhancements that are already working for you. Maybe you need to rearrange a few things. Perhaps a little spring cleaning can help to get these stale areas working for you.

~~~

What would the world be like without any enhancements?
—My friend, Margie Schurman

~~~

Water

Water represents *money*! Positive, physical water can be seen in the form of fountains, aquariums, bowls, ponds and vases. It can be represented by the colour blue, a wavy pattern or a picture with water. Tumbled stones can also represent water or a water feature.

Water is the element associated with the career area. And since water nourishes wood, the family area and the wealth area can benefit also. In business, these water features are intended to create activity and inspire positive energy.

If you choose to use real water in your enhancement, be sure the water is consistently clean and clear. If you'd like to add fish or plants into your space, keep them healthy. For the exact number of fish or plants, you can either choose the number designated to the area (gua) you are enhancing or choose another auspicious number to act as reinforcement.

If you are shopping for a fountain for your desk or reception area, size does matter. Be sure to scale the feature to the space available. It should be considerably smaller than one you choose for your entrance or the garden.

Tip: The number nine is auspicious in feng shui. If you choose to use live fish, koi are the lucky choice. They are also very hardy! Use a ratio of 1:8 when selecting the colour of your fish. Choose one red fish and eight black or one black and eight red. If you desire more fish, choose a multiple of nine and keep the same ratio of colours. (For 27 fish, choose 3 red and 24 black).

If your plumbing is in the area that you are trying to enhance, you need to watch for water—also known as money—running down the drain. Too much water can signify a potential loss of resources. Go back to the basics. Keep the bathroom door closed and the toilet lid down if it is near your office or entrance. If you have a serious concern, you may choose to contact a feng shui consultant in your area. There are other cures available for dealing with these unique issues that require a professional. Check out the IFS Guild for a consultant near you (see Appendix D).

Entrance

The entrance and doorway into your office or cubicle is very significant. The main opening is related to the mouth of the structure, business and operations. If this mouth is blocked in any way, the energy—ch'i—will be stagnant. With an energy block in the office, you could have issues with productivity.

Greet yourself daily with things that are calming and cheerful—a welcoming painting, colourful flowers and a small table to place your computer while you hang up your coat. A crystal chandelier can grace your welcome area by sending little bits of light and energy into all the corners. A solid welcome mat is both grounding and welcoming. This should be in a dark blue or black colour, as this relates to your career security and your interaction with the outside world.

By keeping the entrance clear and accessible, you should be able to invite new opportunities to your door. Stay positive and look for these opportunities. Take a new look at your entrance to the workplace with fresh eyes. Is it fabulous? Do you *want* to go to work? Is your office pulling you back or pushing you toward success?

Dress for Success: Personal Expression

In the corporate world, there is an image that we need to uphold. In every company and every division, there are nuances. Sending the right message is extremely important when you are doing business. Although you need to maintain a corporate image, you can still dress in a way that represents yourself. Dressing for success can be a form of self-expression.

Your choice of clothing gives others a clue about what mood you are in and how you plan to proceed. If you are confident, clothing can help you send that message. I am not talking about brand names, lipstick and bling; although some people feel they need these items to present themselves to the public. The colours you choose to wear can reflect the way you feel about yourself professionally and have an impact on the people you do business with.

I tend to start with black or navy items and then punch it up from there. It will depend on what I am doing that day and who I will be with. I might choose a subtle bit of colour in the form of a soft scarf or a blouse. Other times, when I have larger audience, a jacket with lots of colours makes a bold statement.

Colour therapy works by stimulating your visual synapses and therefore your mind. How do you wish to present yourself today?

Black and White

- If you are selling items like insurance, investments or nontangible services, you may find that darker colours promote trust and insight.
- When dealing with lawyers or bankers, you as the customer may also want to wear more sobering colours. Calm colours can quiet the mind and help you pay attention.
- Black and white can also reflect contemplative and meditative thoughts. Save these for artistic and creative

processes that need a clean canvas in order to build a masterpiece.

If you are looking for work, your clothes may determine your standing. You may need to think out of the box. Black and white can be de-energizing and do not always represent optimism and cooperation. On the other hand, red or another aggressive colour could signal incompatible behaviour for a new team. Try to bring a little bit of green or blue with you, as these colours represent growth and possibilities.

The standard dark power suit for the guys is respected in all sectors. It shows you are grounded, in control and confident. For the ladies, the little black dress does the same thing, as she should always feel comfortable and in control. The gal who shows up to parties and activities in a red dress is the one everyone looks at, as she does stand out. She's on fire. She's out there. She is *hot!* But what would your reaction would be toward a man who showed up to the party wearing a red suit?

Which Colours Are for Me?

- If you wish to increase your productivity, choose a bright-coloured tie, scarf or outfit. This will get people to notice you, keeping you on your toes.
- If you are hoping to increase your popularity, wear peach colours. These relate to freshness, energy and excitement. A rainbow of colours also works well to attract new people into your life.
- If you are trying to stimulate your mind, try wearing something blue, red or purple. These colours reflect inspiration, royalty and higher ground.
- A salesperson for novelty or fun items may choose bright, fun colours to complement the product.
- When selling a more serious product, a bright tie may lighten the mood.

- If you are stuck in a dull grey city for an entire winter, try wearing brighter colours. Bright colours on a particularly bleak day can be uplifting.

A fresh colour in your wardrobe could energize you enough to try something else that is new. Keep those brain synapses firing!

Where Is the Wealth?

Is it really all about the money? Your personal definition of wealth and abundance may be very different from another person's. Success can be registered in many ways and materialize in many forms. Many people seek fulfillment in their positions through the money they earn.

I suggest you be specific and write down your goals, if you haven't done this already. It is time to set your goals in motion. They can be decadent and even unrealistic. They can be tangible or not. They can be anything you want, just be specific. Be sure to date the piece of paper and put it in a safe place—in your desk, under a coaster or taped to the back of a picture frame in your wealth area. You don't *have* to keep the list, but you may want to refer to it at some time in the future.

Be practical but also take a bold step out of your routine and see what happens. What is the worst thing that could happen? If you define your goals, you'll have a chance to achieve them. Is there anything wrong with that?

The energy of feng shui's five elements will strengthen each area of your office and your life. There is no need to go out and spend a lot of money; you have auspicious elements in your home and office right now. Gather the five elements together by using colour, shapes or anything in your imagination. Whatever you choose needs to resonate within yourself.

- A picture or postcard can have all the colours you require.
- A scarf can feature all the shapes and the texture you desire.
- A coffee cup can be filled with all the items you need.
- A glass bowl of coloured stones and a flower can also meet your criteria.

Larger goals require larger enhancements. You may want to focus on a specific area on your desk, and then reinforce that same life area in your office, building or property.

One easy enhancement is a lucky bamboo arrangement. Bamboo is a symbol of good fortune, good health and prosperity. This plant attracts and increases the flow of positive energy through your office or home. A highly resistant, fast-growing plant, it helps the ch'i to flow freely. The arrangement doesn't have to be elaborate; a few stalks can sit modestly on your desktop. You'll often see them gathered in groups for strength.

The arrangement in figure 8.1 is auspicious, as it does represent all five elements:

- The glass vase represents the hard, metal properties.
- The stones in the glass represent earth, grounded and solid.
- The bamboo represents the wood element—tall, green and flourishing.
- The water is the actual water element.
- A red ribbon placed in the arrangement will represent the fire element.

You can place this lucky bamboo anywhere in your home or office for good luck. Just remember to top up the water every week or so.

To reinforce some of these ideas from the earlier chapters, the key element in the wealth area is wood. Green is the enchanted colour of the wood. The colour represents the spring season, life, growth and abundance. At the same time, the auspicious colour to represent wealth is deep red. The feng shui masters call this colour "so red, it is purple." This is the colour of success, vibrancy and royalty. You need to include both the colours red and green in your enhancement. This is another reason why Christmas decorations are especially vibrant. The colours don't always have to be blatantly visible to the masses. You can tuck some of these lucky enhancements in a desk or plant pots or tape them to the bottom of a drawer. You'll know where they are hidden.

You will want to attract richness to your wealth area, not necessarily liquid assets. This is a great place to display things of value to you—antique rugs or furniture, pearls or gems, coins, crystal, carvings or even pictures with a representation of wealth, such as fishing trips or vacations. These choices are very personal.

I can't tell you exactly what to place in this area for enhancement; I can only make suggestions for you to consider. Perhaps you are more comfortable displaying a picture of your hard-earned rewards: a sailboat, vacation home or outlandish purchase. I'm sure you have plenty of remarkable items to choose from.

To make this area more auspicious and to gather more attention, add a large mirror to magnify the wealth. If your goal is cold hard cash, you may want to add a cache of antique coins to your display or even hide them in a plant pot. I've seen fine jewellery hung from a lamp or a vase to reinforce a wealth area.

In extreme cases, people place real paper money into a display or hide it in their wealth area. A note to cash enthusiasts: Apply a little caution when displaying cash in your home. Some visitors may view this as flaunting or tempting, as a client of mine found out. She had paper money tucked in under the runner of her sideboard table. She checked on it periodically, motivating it to work for her. When spring cleaning, she found that three of the bills had been used. Used? Someone must have borrowed the money and not noticed the mint condition of the bills. The perpetrator replaced them with used bills. The mystery remains unsolved, but at least she was paid back.

You should plan on revisiting your wealth area every few weeks to keep things clutter-free and fresh. If you are working in a private space, you can make these enhancements without having to answer to anyone. If you share your space with another or a group, you'll need to be respectful of that. It is interesting to note how many partners have problems with this concept. You may only have to ask your partner one question to get started: "Would it be a problem for you if I enhance our wealth area?"

Real Snapshots

Ellen and Ryan set up a lovely antique chess set in their wealth area. They made a stunning display in the display cabinet in their dining room with a set of red and green place mats and brass treasures. They also placed a case of poker chips at the base of the cabinet. Their *interpretation* of the wealth area was that they were gambling and hoping to cash in on the high stakes sometime soon. Last time I talked with the couple, their investments were doing just fine.

Anna asked me for help after her husband died. She wanted to sell the house but was waiting for the housing market to bounce back. Could I help cheer up the house a little to keep its value from slipping? Her wealth area was the living room, predominantly black, cream and white. Anna initially resisted my attempts to bring in more colour, but I did manage to move some blue pots over to the fireplace hearth (to counter the huge fireplace).

We went through her wardrobe to search for her favourite colours and selected one of her fine silk scarves to drape over the baby grand piano. The scarf brought a nice softness to the piano. Lastly, I found her grandchild's little teddy bear in a basket of toys and placed it on the couch. The teddy bear was wearing a little red sweater that read "Home Sweet Home." Anna was delighted! She feels much better in her home. She can now enjoy her house while waiting for the right time to sell.

James was a little frustrated with his career when I met him. The corporation was reshuffling again, and he was afraid that this was the last rung on the ladder for him. After his wife and I worked through a few enhancements at their home, I went to his office after hours to evaluate his desk and work area. I suggested to James, a department manager working in a high-rise, that he draw a picture of an aquarium on the whiteboard near his desk, with 24 black fish and 3 red fish.

A month later, James received the promotion he deserved, with a nice raise! This fortune was already in motion. The enhancements gave him the attention and focus needed for his promotion to come through. I asked him a few weeks later if the fish were still on his whiteboard, and he replied, "Oh yes, no one has noticed." I think someone noticed.

Sue, a depressed water person, rearranged her wealth area by placing her antique piano and imported rugs in the spare bedroom. She was disappointed a few months later that her bank account didn't suddenly double in size. When I followed up with Sue, I needed to explain to her that she needs to open the door to the bedroom to let in the fresh air and perhaps play the piano. She needed to *enhance the enhancements* in order to keep them from becoming stagnant and stale. Sue also agreed that it was time to work on her helpful-people and health areas. She needs to be in a better frame of mind to recognize and enjoy any wealth opportunities when they arrive on her doorstep.

Author's Notes about the Wealth Area

When I asked my husband the question, "Would it be a problem for you if I enhanced our wealth area?" he was open for change, as long as I promised not to do anything too weird. What we didn't discuss was the definition of weird!

Our wealth area on the main floor is in the dining room. Dining rooms are easy, as they often already have a dining table and chairs made of wood. In our case, the enhancement items chosen were antique rugs, tall plants and floor-to-ceiling draperies. My personal choice for the focal point was two tall hand-carved ebony giraffes that we bought in Africa. They not only represent a once-in-a-lifetime trip, but they are both stunning and exotic for representation in the wealth area.

Last year, for me personally, I made some enhancements in the house with the intention to increase the cash flow. What happened next was I won a year's supply of bread from the local bakery! Yep, 52 loaves of bread! Be careful what you wish for: Bread dough is not the same as cash dough!

By putting attention and focus into your wealth area, you will be more focused on your intention to earn money, spend wisely or rediscover assets that you may have forgotten about. Search your life and seek out your greatest desires. When we deal with the real issues and look at things differently, we open up new definitions of what wealth means to each of us.

Reader Challenge

I challenge you all to take the first step. Start looking at things in your life a bit differently. You can find abundance in your life that you never knew you had. Write down the date and the specifics about how you selected the enhancements to attain your goals, watch the energy patterns shift and then wait for the results. Who knows what opportunities are right around the corner for you?

I look forward to hearing from you! I welcome your comments and questions, and I'm anxious to know what you have done in your own life areas.

-Kathryn
kathryn@kathrynwilking.com
www.kathrynwilking.com

APPENDIX A

More about the Command Position

The Command Position refers back to a Chinese model from the fourth century BC when people were searching for the best place to bury their ancestors. The logic goes as follows:

- *The back of the Command Position* is represented by the image of a tortoise. The back, which you cannot see, is extremely vulnerable. You want to have your back protected and free from fear.
- *The front of the Command Position* is represented by the image of the phoenix, a bird of perpetual inspiration. The eyes need to be in a position to see a clear, unobstructed view. You want to see all that is going on, and you feel inspired when you are able to see a broad panorama.
- *The right side* is represented by the tiger and possesses great strength, but also requires control and restraint. Energies and objects on your right side will need to be close to the ground (regardless of whether you are right—or left-handed), like a tamed wildcat ready to move.
- *The left side* is represented by the dragon. The dragon is far-sighted and very wise. It has a calm, open mind symbolizing our desire to have a broad outlook on life. The dragon can rise above ordinary eye levels, which is why you are advised to place taller items here, on the left side.

These ideas can be relevant in today's world when assessing working and living areas. You can use this model in very practical ways to assess the psychological impact of furniture and the best spot in a room when you eat, sleep and work. Be aware of your surroundings and establish secure locations in which to meet people or handle social settings.

To relate this specifically to your office, you instinctively know when your back is vulnerable. Your visual field cannot see movements and objects behind you. The body requires security and protection, a good reference to the turtle (the rock) that has your back. Check that your back is secure and grounded.

When you look forward, you want to see a clear unobstructed view. A broad panorama can be inspiring and informative. The phoenix, a bird of inspiration, will allow you the opportunity to stretch your goals and soar. Check that your vision is unobstructed.

The tiger on your right side possesses great strength. The energy needs to be carefully controlled; therefore, the objects on this side need to be close to the ground. On your right side, place lower items for support items, file drawers, end tables and meeting tables. Think tiger: unobstructed and ready for action.

The dragon on the left is far-sighted and very stable. This suggests a broader outlook on life and a calm, open mind. This is the side on which to place tall objects that rise above ordinary eye level. Utilize items such as floor lamps, bookcases and tall plants. This gives you security and a working balance. Think dragon: wise, overseeing, in control, a calming force.

Check out all your positions in your life to see if you are in command—sitting at your desk, while you eat, sleeping in the right place, relaxing after work, in the restaurant, the coffee shop, a waiting room. Can you feel the difference after changing the energy in these areas?

APPENDIX B

More about the Ba-gua

The ba-gua, as stated earlier, can have many interpretations in feng shui. This appendix gives you only five (of the many) interpretations for each gua. This is plenty of information to get you moving toward your goals.

The Gua Designations

The knowledge, career and helpful-people areas are situated the closest to the entrance. They are in the location that interacts with people in your daily activities. These areas depend on relationships outside the confines of your home or office to provide fulfilment, education and help.

The family, health and children areas are situated in the center. They are representative of your body and health and extend to your offspring and heritage lines. These can be simple facts—who you are and where you are from.

The wealth, fame and relationship areas go deeper. They are very private and very personal. It is appropriate they are positioned far away from the entrance in relation to the rest of the world. This is where your personal soul and the private, delicate intimacies in life are kept.

The Ba'gua; The nine Life Areas and their Elements.

WEALTH AND ABUNDANCE	FAME	RELATIONSHIPS
• Represents: Wealth and prosperity • Shape: Tall, columns • Colours: Purple, red, green • Element: Wood • Number: 4	• Represents: Reputation and achievements • Shape: Triangle, sharp things • Colours: Red • Element: Fire • Number: 9	• Represents: Love, marriage and partnerships • Shape: Squares and rectangles • Colours: Red, pink • Element: Earth • Number: 2
FAMILY	**HEALTH**	**CHILDREN & CREATIVITY**
• Represents: Heritage and belonging • Shape: Tall, columns • Colours: Green • Element: Wood • Number: 3	• Represents: Everything • Colours: Yellow and earth tones • Element: Earth • Number: 5	• Represents: Creative influences • Shape: Oval, round • Colours: Grey, white, metallic • Element: Metal • Number: 7
KNOWLEDGE AND WISDOM	**CAREER AND LIFE PATH**	**HELPFUL PEOPLE AND TRAVEL**
• Represents: Knowing and self cultivation • Shape: Square and rectangle • Colours: Blue • Element: Earth • Number: 8	• Represents: Life's path • Shape: Wavy • Colours: Black, dark blues • Element: Water • Number: 1	• Represents: Helpful exchanges • Shape: Oval, round • Colours: Grey, white, metallic • Element: Metal • Number: 6

Line up your desk, doorway or entrance with this edge.

The numbers in the ba-gua grid are auspicious to their own life areas. Numerology has its own school and has multiple levels of interpretation. You can utilize the numbers in each gua while arranging plants, flowers, pictures and more in the areas you want to enhance.

Floor Plans

If you have a large area to assess, it will be easier if you lay out the ba-gua on a floor plan. Many floor plans are somewhat irregular, so here is how to proceed:

- First, line up the ba-gua with the entrance or main doorway as previously shown.
- Line up the side edges of the ba-gua, one side at a time. Draw the edge of the ba-gua in line with the wall that is the longest on that side. Sounds a bit complicated, but it isn't; refer to the figure 9.1 in this appendix.
- Draw the interior ba-gua lines. Evenly space three squares wide and three squares long within the floor plan.

There will be areas of the floor plan that fall outside of your ba-gua and areas within the ba-gua that the floor plan doesn't cover. These are your bonus and missing spaces. If you have space outside of the ba-gua, congratulations! This is a bonus for whatever section of the ba-gua it's attached to. Take advantage of it by keeping it clean and working for you. There is one example of a missing area shown in the floor plan in figure 2.4. For spaces within the ba-gua that are missing from your floor plan:

- Place a mirror on the shorter wall in order to push it back to lengthen the room.
- Place a picture of plants or flowers on the wall to help it grow.
- Go back to the enhancements in chapter 8; anything that can draw attention to this area is good. Get creative with

this area by trying wind chimes, hanging crystals and floor plants with flowers to expand the space.

- Sometimes you can cure this missing area from outside the room. On the outside of the room or building, find the intersecting point where you can square off your space. Mark this site securely with something relatively permanent, such as a large rock, flagpole, garden stake, light or tree.
- Failing the option to dig up your hallway or neighbour's office, square off the area with a cupboard, filing cabinet or floor plant. I've seen people set designs in a carpet or even mark their space with an overhead visual such as a crystal. Time to get creative if you feel this is a weak area for you.

If you have other issues and do not know where to start, please contact a certified feng shui consultant to help you.

BIBLIOGRAPHY

Beinfield, Harriet, and Efrem Korngold. *Between Heaven and Earth: A Guide to Chinese Medicine.* New York: Ballantine Books, 1992.

Chuen, Lam Kam. *The Personal Feng Shui Manual: How to Develop a Healthy and Harmonious Lifestyle.* New York: Henry Holt and Company, 1998.

Mitchell, Shawne. *Exploring Feng Shui: Ancient Secrets and Modern Insight for Love, Joy, and Abundance.* Pompton Plains, NJ: Career Press, 2002.

Rossbach, Sarah. *Interior Design with Feng Shui.* New York: Penguin Books, 2000.

Rossbach, Sarah, and Lin Yun. *Living Color: Master Lin Yun's Guide to Feng Shui and the Art of Color.* New York: Kodansha America, 1994.

FURTHER READING AND WEBSITES

Books

- *Clear Your Clutter with Feng Shui* by Karen Kingston
- *The Western Guide to Feng Shui for Prosperity* by Terah Kathryn Collins
- *Workstation Radiation: How to Reduce Electromagnetic Radiation Exposure from Computers, TV Sets, and Other Sources* by Lucinda Grant
- *Living Safely with Electromagnetic Radiation: A Complete Guide for Protecting Your Health* by Jim Waugh
- *Zapped: Why Your Cell Phone Shouldn't Be Your Alarm Clock and 1,268 Ways to Outsmart the Hazards of Electronic Pollution* by Ann Louise Gittleman
- *The Electrical Sensitivity Handbook: How Electromagnetic Fields (EMFs) Are Making People Sick* by Lucinda Grant
- *The Power of Money: How You See Money Is How You See Yourself* by Sonia Nadina Haynes

Websites and Newsletters

- International Feng Shui Guild, ifsguild.org
- Sacred Lotus School of Feng Shui, fengshuiclasses.ca
- The EMR Network, emrnetwork.org
- Institute of Feng Shui and Geopathology, instituteoffengshui.com
- Health Action Network Society (HANS), hans.org

- EMF Protection (personal protection items), emfblues.com
- EMF Protection Store (cell phone protection), emfprotectionstore.com
- Less EMF (protective fabrics, books, meters), lessemf.com

ABOUT THE AUTHOR

 Kathryn Wilking has been involved with Interior Design and the Home Improvement Industry for more than 25 years, and is a specialist in Paints and Coatings. She is also a certified Gold Level Feng Shui Consultant and Real Estate Stager. Her goal is to create safe and happy environments for the home and office.

Kathryn is a people person, adapting with the changing times. She first graduated with a Diploma in Communications and Labour Management from Niagara College, followed by Certificates in International Trade and Women in Technical Trades. As a project consultant, Kathryn has opened, moved and renovated retail stores and offices, and also developed a technical catalogue for kitchen design. Through these multi-faceted experiences, she has observed behavioural and design challenges in a wide range of business settings, and has developed a unique approach to promoting harmony in the workplace.

Feng shui became a personal lifestyle in 1998 when Kathryn and her son settled in with her new husband and step-son. The puzzle was how to blend the two families together, and she used feng shui to help with the colour, organization and decorating challenges. That successful makeover sparked Kathryn to learn more about feng shui; a little bit each year, trying a few things, changing things, and adapting these principles for use in her personal lifestyle. After 10 years, she decided to complete formal feng shui certification. In this, her first book, Practical Feng Shui for the Office, Kathryn shares her knowledge and gives you the tools to solve your puzzles.

A transplant from Niagara in 2006, Kathryn now resides with her husband in the Lower Mainland of B.C. in Canada.

CPSIA information can be obtained at www.ICGtesting.com
Printed in the USA
LVOW060851100713

342097LV00001B/2/P